# CONSTRUCTING BUILDINGS
## FOR MODEL RAILWAYS

# CONSTRUCTING BUILDINGS FOR MODEL RAILWAYS

An Illustrated Guide to the Process

**David Ashwood**

&

The Market Deeping Model Railway Club, CIO

AN IMPRINT OF PEN & SWORD BOOKS LTD.
YORKSHIRE – PHILADELPHIA

First published in Great Britain in 2023 by
Pen and Sword Transport
An imprint of
Pen & Sword Books Ltd.
Yorkshire - Philadelphia

Copyright © David Ashwood, 2023

ISBN 978 1 39909 492 4

The right of David Ashwood to be identified as author of this work has been asserted by him in accordance with the Copyright, Designs and Patents Act 1988.

A CIP catalogue record for this book is available from the British Library.

All rights reserved. No part of this book may be reproduced or transmitted in any form or by any means, electronic or mechanical including photocopying, recording or by any information storage and retrieval system, without permission from the Publisher in writing.

Typeset in 11.5/14 Palatino
by SJmagic DESIGN SERVICES, India.

Printed and bound by Printworks Global Ltd, London/Hong Kong.

Pen & Sword Books Ltd incorporates the imprints of Pen & Sword Books Archaeology, Atlas, Aviation, Battleground, Discovery, Family History, History, Maritime, Military, Naval, Politics, Railways, Select, Transport, True Crime, Fiction, Frontline Books, Leo Cooper, Praetorian Press, Seaforth Publishing, Wharncliffe and White Owl.

For a complete list of Pen & Sword titles please contact

PEN & SWORD BOOKS LIMITED
George House, Units 12 & 13, Beevor Street, Off Pontefract Road,
Barnsley, South Yorkshire, S71 1HN, England
E-mail: enquiries@pen-and-sword.co.uk
Website: www.pen-and-sword.co.uk

or

PEN AND SWORD BOOKS
1950 Lawrence Rd, Havertown, PA 19083, USA
E-mail: Uspen-and-sword@casematepublishers.com
Website: www.penandswordbooks.com

# Contents

1 Introduction .................................................................................................... 7

2 Pre-built ......................................................................................................... 13

3 Paper and Card Kits ...................................................................................... 17

4 Plastic Kits ..................................................................................................... 28

5 Wood, MDF, Resin and Metal Kits .............................................................. 34

6 Freestyle and Scratch Building .................................................................... 47

7 Lighting Your Buildings ............................................................................... 59

8 Railway Buildings ......................................................................................... 66

9 Rural Buildings ............................................................................................. 73

10 Urban Buildings ............................................................................................ 80

11 Industrial Buildings ...................................................................................... 91

Why We 'Do' Model Railways ......................................................................... 101

# 1
# Introduction

As with our initial publication, *How to Build a Model Railway*, we have taken the opportunity of incorporating previously unpublished images to give a frisson of prototype activity. Here, proving that you can have a layout with a true minimum of railway infrastructure, is AC Cars Railbus W79977 at Boscarne exchange platform on 18 August 1966, just prior to closure. (*Online Transport Archive Meredith 629-9*)

*The past is a foreign country, they do things differently there*

L.P. Hartley

The Market Deeping Model Railway Club (MDMRC) was formed in 1976, the year *Concorde* took to the skies. The Club, in common with all of its ilk, is a thriving social ecosystem of like-minded railway modellers, with a desire to learn, share, specialise and display the end results to the public at exhibitions. The pictures on the following pages are taken from a combination of Club and home layouts belonging to members, and represent the broad spectrum of this hobby, from the smallest display, through child-friendly layouts to larger, longer-term builds.

Like so many that exist in the United Kingdom, this Club has an interesting mix of contributing careers, a can-do attitude and a structure of 'officers' that can cope with planning and budgeting through to handling the most unexpected of circumstances. Indeed, the Club would have been termed as 'proficient but unexceptional' among its peers, until disaster struck on the night of 17 May 2019.

The Annual Model Railway Show was set up at a school in the idyllic town of Stamford, Lincolnshire, on a Friday night, ready for an early start the next morning. All hands were on deck, a hive of activity after the school closed for the day. Layouts were set up and tested, 'position one' rolling stock put in place. Traders arrived and their wares were set out ready to sell on their displays.

During the night the school sports hall was invaded, and an extensive spree of vandalism occurred.

At 6:30 am the school caretaker with the author and his wife, who were simply expecting to make the morning's breakfast rolls, instead opened up to discover most of the contents had been comprehensively reduced to matchwood. Our own layouts, those of fellow clubs and the traders' stalls were all demolished.

It was the last thing you would expect to see. In some cases, twenty-five years of work were gone; kindly men over seventy were in tears. The Club and all others present experienced shock, anger and disbelief. That Saturday afternoon was spent with brooms and dustbins, and we wondered just where we would go to cope with the damage and loss of Club earnings. We decided to set up a £500 'Just Giving' request online to offset losses.

During the following week, news of the vandalism was flashed around the world,

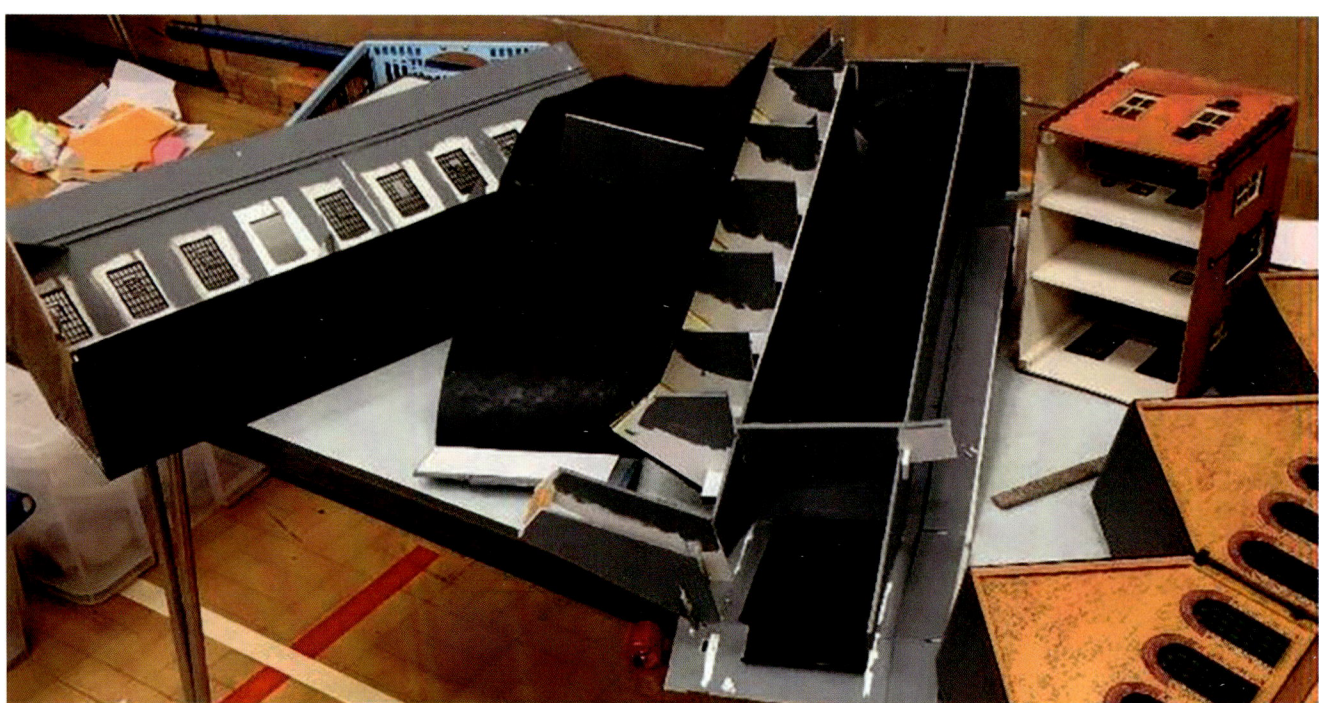

Close up of a small part of the overall damage in the school sports hall. Whole layouts and trade displays were overturned and badly damaged, some destroyed. Much just went out in black bin bags that afternoon, far beyond saving, other parts became potential donors for future projects. (*MDMRC*)

Aftermath. Following the show disaster there was a worldwide media uptake on the story. In itself this alleviated some of the shock experienced and pitched the Club team into a new world never before experienced. Seen here is preparation for a BBC news segment recording – we had promised a local literary festival that we would attend a venue. We did so with a hurried resurrection of our long-stored OO Cannons Cross layout and another N gauge layout borrowed from a club member. (*MDMRC*)

seizing the common imagination. Club members appeared on television and radio. Our one operable locomotive, taken from a raffle prize, was set up on our Club's test track to show some background movement.

Within a day, members of the rail modelling fraternity, wargamers, the general public, people with fond memories of their grandfathers' past, provided kind words, and donations of all kinds poured in. From Miniatur Wonderland of Hamburg and Sir Rod Stewart through to children's pocket money and a lady from Japan apologising for her English. It should be realised that there was not only the financial investment, but the irreplaceable time and devotion of past and older members, ideas, aspirations, discovery – all had been lost.

As a result, the Club decided to form into a charity to process those donations appropriately, curate a historical collection of assets representing the evolution of the hobby in Britain and elsewhere, promote clubs for local children and assist other local good causes. Good can come from bad, eventually. Our share of profit from this book goes directly back into the charity fund.

This publication is aimed at sharing the Club members' experience and skills involved in constructing model buildings, an integral part of most railway layouts.

The author cut his teeth with products purchased from Teddington Model Supplies, a fairy-tale turreted building perched atop the railway bridge in that locale. That particular shop is alas now long gone to the model railway in the sky. There, a chain-smoking Burma war veteran fronted the railway and accessory kits side, and a rotund jolly chap in glasses presided over displays of tanks, planes and gliders (the shop always carried a heavy aroma of Woodbines and doped tissue paper). There were sporadic appearances of Airfix and Kitmaster kits with their wonderfully illustrated boxes. It was never a smooth supply. Early cardboard and paper building kits appeared alongside the trusty Merit accessories brand. These were eventually joined by Superquick, enabling detailed constructions in cardboard.

Lessons were learned with the card medium. The correct glue to use was a fundamental one. You could use cow gum or bone glue as a harmless adhesive, only to discover that on a hot day it all fell apart with stretchy tendrils. Copydex always smelt of fish and Gloy never came out of the bottle well, especially with the change from rubber to plastic bottle dispensers.

If you spilt it and let it harden you could never break it up. I still have Gloy amber-like deposits in wooden trays containing my childhood Hornby Dublo tinplate.

Having perhaps portrayed myself as a dinosaur, I am fortunately also a member of a club that looks forward and uses innovative techniques. It maintains standards, and shares skills, as well as cherishing the older, trusted approaches to modelling. A subtle blend built of experience, new technology and still with a feeling in the background of the comfy leather armchairs and pipes of those trailblazers that passed long before.

Books such as this cannot exist in pure isolation, they serve as a launch pad for greater things – reading periodical magazines, using the library service, searching the internet, visiting model shows and asking questions, to see what can be done. Model shop owners and exhibitors get lonely, they love to talk. Above all enjoy yourself in discovering the pleasure of a perfect little world where the trains will always run on time.

Our thanks go to Pen & Sword Books for taking the brave move to present another facet of the modelling hobby beyond the military and technical. Their extensive coverage is sure to tempt anyone that has looked twice longingly at a museum exhibit or a model kit.

Thank you to Alan Hancock and Peter Davies for proofreading and members of the Market Deeping Club for their kind assistance and willingness to share and advise.

## Decisions and Basic Equipment

While making buildings for a model is for some a means to an end, for many it is, or will become, a labour of love. Starting off correctly, building one's skills, using the correct tools, avoiding dead ends and indeed avoiding personal injury will introduce you to the hobby and keep you interested long into the future.

Decide in which scale to build. For some this is determined by a pre-existing train set, for others it is a 'greenfield site'. Scale will determine how fiddly components will be when constructing and the space required by the resultant buildings. If stations and towns are secondary to your desire to run trains, this not a problem. But if you want to run a railway through the 'landscape', the upfront decision making can be important.

Which materials will you build with? There are a variety of manufacturers and materials to choose from. Potentially, you can expand your skills over time by taking simple kits in a particular material as a start point and then progressing. Pre-printed paper or card material removes the need to paint a finish later and achieves comparatively quick results at a decent cost. Embossed plastics, resin, plaster and metals give another level of detail but need the artistic flourish to complete.

If you plan well, you will be able to position your earlier attempts at layout locations that will hide minor mistakes, hence retaining your investment in both cash and time. If all else fails keep early structures in the spares box to cannibalise later in your modelling career.

Always remember for whom the models are intended. If you are detailing a layout for the kids, build cheaper kits and involve them where possible. There will be breakages and it pays not to be precious about the resulting buildings. If the work is for yourself, you can step back, invest in some useful tools beyond the breadboard and penknife, and enjoy the constructional experience.

N gauge or 2mm scale. You can fit a lot in, costs can be low, but this scale boggles the eyes and fingers and requires great dexterity.

OO gauge or 4mm scale. Most train sets are sold in this scale and initial forays into building will come on the back of expansion from the basics. Lots to choose from over a wide variety of materials.

O gauge or 7mm scale. Before the Second World War, this was the most popular scale with children. More recently it has seen a resurgence with adults and there is now a better provision of buildings. It swallows the available space, but the detail level can be very high.

So, from experience, what generic toolbox have people ended up using? Multiple self-healing cutting mats which prove better than a wood board or a single large mat. Oilcloth to cover a table and prevent damage from glues or paint. A metal ruler for folding against or cutting carefully along. A retractable blade craft knife and many replacement blades (a sharp unbroken blade is a must). A 90° modeller's/engineer's set square to keep those corners crisp. A fine-toothed craft saw to get those pernickety bits of wood or plastic cut neatly. Dedicated scissors (don't fight over the kitchen drawer contents), both the fine cut and bone-cutter type. Tweezers are really useful, especially the crossed-over self-closing ones. Finally, a magnifying lens, either for your head or the table-clamp type, with a light source, is a godsend even if your eyes are good. You'll find your own favourite extras over time – for example, Blu Tack to hold things in place when gluing, polystyrene offcuts to use with cocktail sticks to pin out components as they adhere, low-tack masking tape to join corners temporarily.

Plan view of Butterwick, an O gauge layout. Cut-outs, odd angles, a mix of scratch building, MDF kits, resin and scrap box parts all contribute to fitting a lot in without it appearing crowded. Every encroachment towards the track needs testing for clearances to avoid conflicts. The coal stage was 1mm out on a corner with a Class 08 diesel shunter, but an 0-6-0 Jinty tank engine worked just fine. This required some tricky trimming in situ despite repeated cross-checking.

# 2
# Pre-built

When first venturing into model railway infrastructure, most people normally purchase a pre-built platform and station building. The operating experience is always better with somewhere to stop. Seen here on 12 July 1967 are the very tidy platforms of Rock Ferry station which had just become a full terminus following the closure of Birkenhead Woodside station. Diesel trains from Chester and Helsby would arrive here allowing interchange to the Mersey electric trains on the far side, where a Class 503 unit can be seen. Today this infrastructure is much reduced. (*BRB Derby*)

Originally railway buildings and accessories were extremely basic, made from tinplate or wood blocks with printed paper finishes, as well as cheaper ersatz home-built examples gifted from father to son.

Over the years the quality and detail of the available pre-built lineside structures have kept pace with changes in rolling stock. They have also benefited from the increase in disposable income over time to support the development of a wide selection of models.

Although this book covers the physical construction of model buildings, incorporating pre-built models or using these as a basis for expanding your building stock is no sin. They can be a stopgap or an end point. It all depends on what your overall requirements are.

There is a lively second-hand market in such models, some pristine, others requiring renovation. There is fun to be had in improving a 'fixer-upper' purchased from a model show or online. This reflects the real-life trend with unimproved properties and their popularity on television.

*Below*: At rear, a pristine Hornby Dublo station model. These metal castings of the 1950s were robust and long lived, both in production terms and in the hands of children. Nearer examples: some manufacturers brought out wood and paper variations and other more artisan models were made to save money when times were tight. Detail, colours and accuracy are a little wayward to the modern eye. To the youngsters of the day, however, they were the 'bee's knees'.

With some imagination, second-hand pre-built structures can be given a new lease of life. Here the standard die-cast Hornby Dublo D1 signal cabin of the 1950s is shown as a boxed example, and one that, judging by the roughly applied metallic paint, was disfigured by a child in the 1970s. Fortunately the painted overcoat reacted well to a water-soluble paint stripper. Any hope of returning to original colouration was lost, therefore making it a guilt-free candidate for conversion. After a little keying of the stripped surfaces using wet and dry fine grade paper, it was soap-washed and then oversprayed with a grey automotive primer to act as a sound foundation. Interestingly, in primed form the pleasing detail of the casting is appreciated for the first time. These diecast models are extremely robust. This example represents (in format if not in colour) something akin to LNER post-war signal boxes, such as South Doncaster (replaced subsequently by the Grantham to Doncaster power signal box), plus some freestyle modernism and a bit of wartime reinforced ARP design, all mixed together.

The same signal box transformed into a 1930s' London Transport style control room of the Holden and Pick architectural genre. Utilising printed brick paper and roof texture from coarse sandpaper sheet, the signal box quickly becomes a valued asset again. As with all mini projects part of the fun comes from the research, from direct prototypes to 'what if' freelance.

Restoring a building and reglazing requires a bit of forethought in process, especially where windows are out of normal finger reach. The Dublo castings were never glazed even though transparent plastics were used in the carriages. Use was made of clear plastic from recycling a bath set raffle prize. Self-closing tweezers are very useful – squeeze to release. The bit of meat skewer (or alternatively a cocktail stick) is to take beads of adhesive into the right locations around the inside of the window frames.

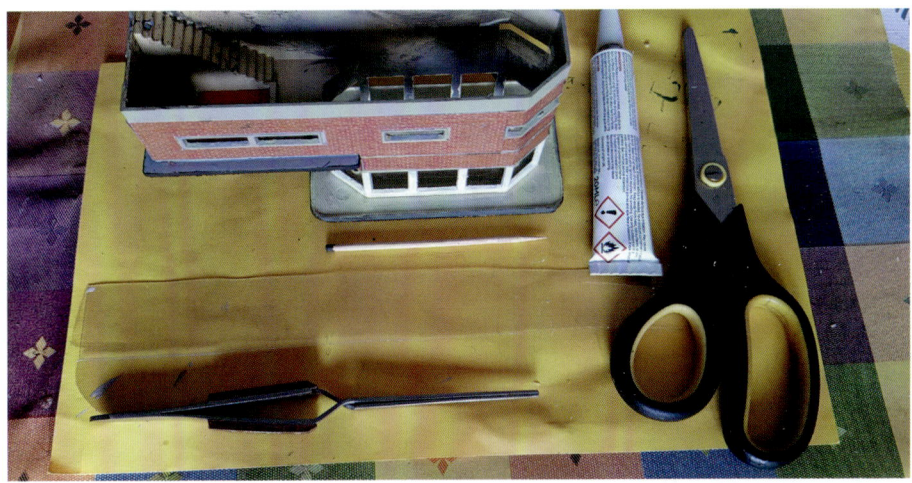

A very sharp knife is used to score the soft transparent plastic so that it will fit around the inside of window apertures. If you try to bend the plastic without this it will stretch, becoming translucent along the bend line, to the detriment of your finished work. Modern general purpose gel adhesives do not fog this soft clear plastic and should last a long time with a strong bond.

Finally completed and offered up as a control room on a static model of a 'what if' London Transport station. A detailed electronic control panel type interior was included plus LED lighting, and some 3D-printed extras such as control boxes. What was perhaps destined for the bin is now integrated and seeing a second life. It will be weathered and blended in with the general scene so that all the buildings feel cohesive. In the modern days of recycling, it is gratifying to take an old toy and make it into a model.

The humble signal box has evolved over time since the die-cast example.

*Left:* Hornby (Triang) R145 with a modern plastic moulded cabin. Unpainted and with bright plastic colouration.
*Right:* A highly detailed Bachman model which uses state-of-the-art production techniques but has a greater fragility in the hands of the younger enthusiast.

# 3
# Paper and Card Kits

A plethora of quality paper and card kits exists on the market today and can enable the prospective builder to choose from a wide variety of options at a reasonable price. A comparatively fast population of a model layout can be undertaken at a budget to supplement the often complex plans of trackwork. Seen here is Newton Abbott station and diesel depot on Wednesday 17 August 1966. Class 43 Warship D836, *Powerful*, showcases its hydraulic transmission technology. On the same day NASA launched *Pioneer 7* which intercepted Halley's comet in 1986. By May 1971 *Powerful* had prematurely passed into railway history. (*Meredith 629-2 Online Transport Archive*)

Model railway shows are great places to get an idea of the variety of available kits for your model railway or town. Seen here is the Indigo Works stand at a show in 2019 with entry-level O gauge kits. You can get hints and tips from stallholders as well as purchase or order whatever catches your eye. If you have never made a building kit before, commence with entry-level kits to get the feel for things. Even if you would not incorporate the finished construction on your own layout, you gain good skills ready for the more complex model builds in card or other media.

## Entry-level Kits

Everybody has to start somewhere to build up skills and produce a finished item without being dispirited or put off by the process.

There are kits in each scale that can be regarded as 'entry level'. They have a degree of realism to them, and can be made without too much frustration. They may exist on a layout for some years if care is taken with their storage. It is recommended that adult and child alike pass through this layer as 'training'. It helps to get used to the type of instructions given and gain a feel for the 3D nature of the build-up.

Such kits may not last too long on a layout, getting damaged or superseded over time. However, as they involve a lower financial outlay, they are ideal to boost confidence and, rather as with jigsaw puzzles, consequently allow the move on to the more challenging builds.

For some, the build challenge is an end in itself, each successive card-based kit having a greater complexity and introducing the ability to tailor to your own needs on a layout. For children, initial adult supervision can be slowly relaxed as they become adept in the process and look forward to the next build.

These entry-level kits were purchased for a Club display stand with the aim of introducing children aged eight-plus to construction. Our desire was to demonstrate the concept of safe 3D building from a flat pack without cutting or the use of glue, but still requiring first-time guidance from an adult.

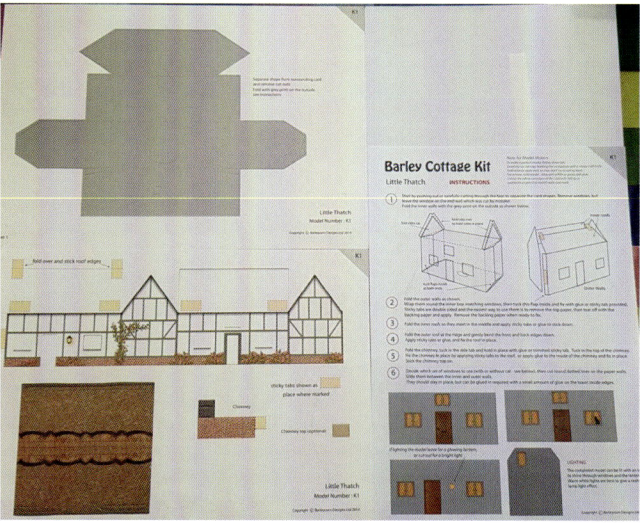

This type of kit is ideal as a starter: thin card with twin wall carcase construction that is pressed out from a pre-embossed fret and has push-outs allowing for illumination. No glue or sticky tape was needed as adhesive pads were provided as a part of the kit pack.

Releasing the building from the retaining fret. Easy to do, allowing adult and child to share the activity while working from a provided sequence of operations. It is as well to get good habits in place early. Many is the 'grown up' that leaps into a kit only to discover that parts A and C have been glued forgetting the essential part B that fell on the floor. (The reader may spot that some past experience is being related to here – it was the Superquick A10 terminal station at age 12 many years ago.)

Experimenting with the degree of fold and whether a joint requires to be generally loose or tight according to the plans.

# PAPER AND CARD KITS • 19

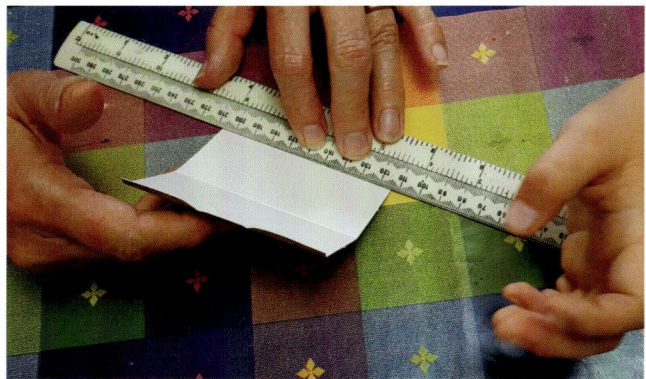

Reminiscent of the card kits of the 1950s and 60s but with modern print standards. These kits have guiding lines but no embossing/scoring for folds. Encourage use of a straight edge such as a ruler to ensure smooth folds.

First ever model completed successfully. No scissors or glue involved and an experiment that worked well.

The finished kit illuminated by use of a torch as a light source to show how even a simple kit can give a decent degree of realism.

This Bilt-Eezi George Inn paper kit is stuck over an artist's fibre card framework as this material is very stable and warp resistant. This enables a mixture of self-building, combined with pre-printed detailed timbering and tiling to complete an inexpensive but detailed result. Paper-based kits are readily available to purchase or buy online and print out yourself.

The building includes interior details so that views through the windows are extremely realistic – in this example even going as far as an inglenook fireplace, plus of course the bar.

Introducing a technological innovation to making your own paper kits. Here the Google Sketchup CAD (computer-aided design) product has been used by Ken Bonham to 'render' surfaces from photographs of a real church. Built over a card frame this is a 3D representation of photographs from different faces, scaled to size for printing.

## Card Kit Building Tips

- Read the instructions fully, don't jump straight in.
- Invest in a self-healing soft cutting mat of A4 size minimum from a craft supplier. You can use a smooth kitchen safety glass cutting board for precise cutting if wished.
- Have a metal ruler to cut against or to fold with.
- Use a glue suitable for card that dries clear – either a general adhesive or PVA. You can use a match or cocktail stick to transport the glue to detail areas.
- Consider using a dressmaker's pin in the top of the glue tube. Crimp the tip of the nozzle with it in and create a smaller aperture to deliver adhesive. The pin will also prevent the nozzle from becoming blocked.
- Invest in a decent craft knife with a very sharp blade and a cutting point. Don't compromise.
- When cutting, be careful of personal injury. Use the knife at a shallow angle away from the hand and body, to slice rather than tear a cut.
- When pushing out cardboard apertures or releasing from a sheet, use the knife to free up corners and prevent tearing.
- Use extra scrap card to support walls beyond those supports supplied to prevent warping over time.
- When gluing windows into place, add side supports using card of similar thickness. This can then have an extra layer of card to fix the window and prevent damage on the layout (faux curtain card, if used, will do the same).
- Ordinary kitchen towels make great net curtains.
- Determine whether you wish to have open windows when cutting transparencies and whether you are overlapping sash windows.
- Black card stuck to and protruding from the front underside of a roofline fools the eye and makes a great gutter effect.

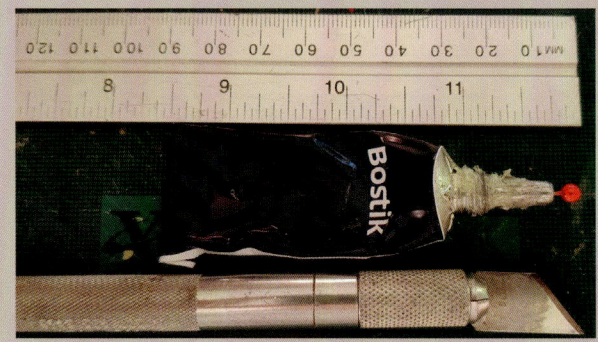

Cardboard media is often chosen for speed of construction, relative simplicity of building and overall value for money. However, there are times when alternative mediums should be considered, as demonstrated by this Greystones Farmhouse built many years ago. If exposed to daylight, certain colours will fade – bright reds first, and blues slowly following. The underlying card and paper will also darken with chemical weathering.

Effects of exposure to damp and excessive heat. Even if you have used an external PVA-type adhesive, the cardboard itself will pick up excessive damp and start to warp. This building was used on an unlined loft layout tucked away in the eaves. When it was foggy outside there was high humidity inside. The summer heat aided delamination as well as weakening the cardboard structure.

The glazing was held in place by Sellotape or similar. Initially this would have been a clean and easy adhesion. After the passage of years however, the glue goes solid and darkens in hue. The windows are very easy to damage, and some fall out on their own. Admittedly these were saved, cleaned up a little and used on a plastic kit that had lost its own glazing. The rest of the building alas went to the big layout in the sky. Using clear glue and then a paper overlap frame to secure glazing to the board inside the building ensures a longer-term life.

Consistent compression when folding and gluing ensures a good long-term bond between surfaces. Clothes pegs are invaluable here.

Kits often come with compartmentalisation to add to strength. Beneficially, this also allows room-by-room lighting if desired.

The humble card kit can be weathered, and details added for extra realism beyond the base model.

*Above and below*: Low relief OO Metcalfe kits being altered to represent the 100-year lifespan of a single building. Far left is 1901 after initial building and is closest to the base kit in nature. Feeling clean and simplistic, housing developments are cohesive and similar. Next is the building in 1941, during wartime, with the windows taped against bomb blast. Maintenance and pride begin to dip and maturing gardens develop. By the early 1970s we have the onward march of DIY and the trend of dividing houses into rented flats or rooms. By this time, inner-urban housing stock is going down in quality and the rot seemingly setting in. In 2001 the complexity of infrastructure grows and there is large scale replacement of doors and windows. Modifications to homes and shops gather pace, external clutter is everywhere – it is the death of homogeneous properties. Tweak your kits to represent your target period and see the benefits on your layout.

## A Retaining Wall for Euston Station

This is a worked example for the 4mm OO club model of Euston Station set in the year 1875. While the majority of buildings on this 100sq ft-plus (9.2sq m) station cutaway are scratch built, certain areas of infrastructure are required that would benefit from an off-the-shelf addition.

Historically, in the north-eastern corner of the old station cutting, a carriage shed was demolished and much of the area infilled to form the back lot of the Railway Clearing House (RCH) (effectively the home of standards, communication and billing for all the different railway companies that existed at the time). The RCH building itself will appear later in this book as a scratch-build example.

A Metcalfe kit for a brickwork retaining wall with supporting piers and arches looked similar to old photographs of the newly northward extended platform 1 of the station. In those days up to three trains of four-wheel carriages would stand here in the rush hour waiting to be assisted up the 'Grand Excavation' of the 1 in 85 Camden incline.

Colour images taken ninety years later just prior to the demolition of the old station show very polluted brickwork that had lost its initial bright colouration. Since the model is set just after the creation of this wall, the engineers blue and London stock red brick would be as fresh as portrayed in the kit without the need for any weathering.

# PAPER AND CARD KITS • 23

Examples of railway infrastructure kits from the club kit box. The cardboard kits of today vary from the basics of a station platform through to tunnel mouths, retaining walls and station buildings for villages and towns. These are printed to modern standards and cut/embossed for folding and removal from the fret. Many have high detail laser-cut board for canopy details, railings and capitals. Long gone are the days of using balsa wood, shoeboxes, shirt packing or the rear card of an A4 school writing pad, then gluing on an offset lithograph muted colour paper sheet.

Board six of Euston Station is seen perched precariously on the back of the trusty Land Rover ersatz workbench. It is a wet and cold May day at the end of the series of Covid-19 isolation and distancing lockdowns. The end of the broad platform 2/3 is in the middle. The red lines mark the desired position of the retaining wall for platform 1. The scratch-built Ampthill Square bridge is in its approximate position leading to the fiddle yard.

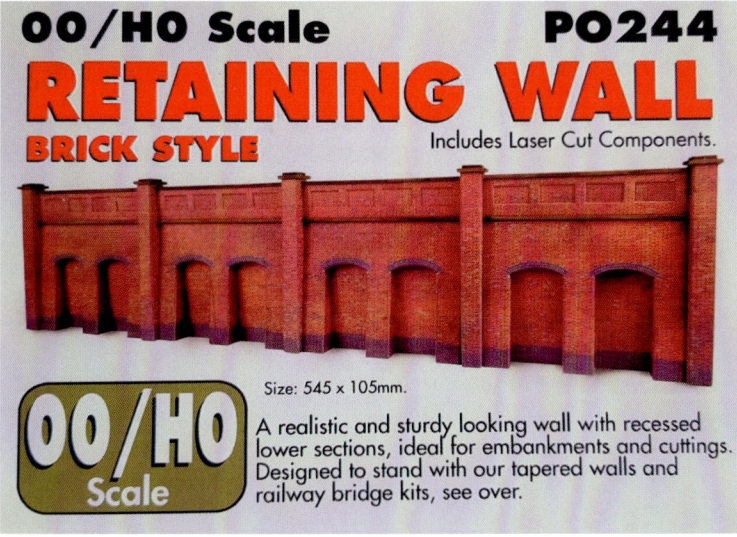

The donor kit pulled from the club kit box. Fortunately, although previously opened, nothing was missing. Always be very aware, when purchasing card kits, that they should be in undamaged boxes or packets, not having been subjected to damp or curving through inappropriate storage. If you have one you have badly stored yourself then a few nights under your collection of railway books should sort things out. This helps to justify having built up a large reference library.

Checking through against the instructions to ensure completeness and lack of any damage before removing any pieces. The temptation is always to dive straight in – resist it.

*Above left*: Grey constructional card fretwork used for the unseen stiffeners and supports. The snap blade type of knife proves very useful for this work. If blunt, then just break off the blade end to re-establish a sharpness that can follow the cut lines neatly and safely.

*Above right*: Most card kits have a long side that is embossed but not fully cut. It requires knifework to release. Beware of accidentally cutting a fold line. If you do, it's not a disaster and can normally be saved by gluing a paper hinge on the rear of the line. Once upon a time I used my mother's spare (best) breadboard as a cutting mat. Today I use a self-healing craft mat. Such mats not only self-heal where you cut into them, but also slow the blade down, preventing 'runaways'. The cut marks disappear, leaving a level surface.

*Left*: A nice touch with this kit range is the inclusion of spare brick- or stonework. Ideal in this case for the wall recurve required on the platform.

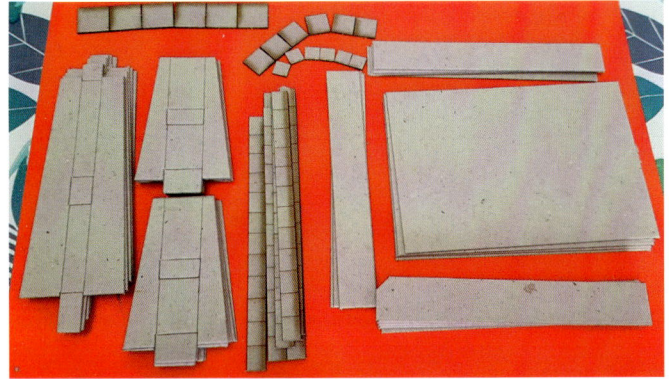 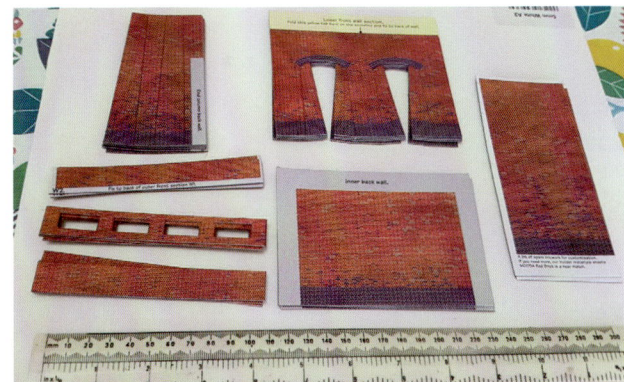

*Above left and above right*: The instructions encourage detaching parts and placing in a 'building site' of components. This gives pre-knowledge of the shape and sequence of the parts and encourages a logical build sequence.

**Adhesives.** There is a wide choice of adhesives that can be used in the build of card kits. Some opt for a combination of double-sided tape and dots of glue, which need no weighting or securing to remain in place during the drying process. The downside here is that after a couple of years the efficacy of the tape glue layer reduces. From personal experience I recommend three adhesive types for use with card. **PVA white wood glue** dries matt-transparent, but has a slow 'stick' (drying) time. This glue can be brushed onto the surfaces to be stuck. **Aliphatic resin** is a high-quality wood glue with strong end adhesion and a mid-stick time. It can be dotted into place. **Clear general gel glue**, such as Uhu or Bostik, provides quick adhesion, meaning there is little time spare to make adjustments.

Glue pattern technique on fold areas. PVA glue can be generally pasted onto the back of card with a brush. Resins are generally dotted in place. With gel glues, run a seam around the outside, close to the edge (think of preventing the bead from extruding out from the edge when pressed) and then swirl a line on the inner surface. You have to be quick and confident as the glue soaks quickly into the raw card.

As with fold overlaps, the gluing of board sections requires a consistent approach. With PVA and resin glue, a wide spread should be made on one face with brush or scrap cardboard. With clear glue, as shown, a bead and infill is needed to ensure a good bond without weakness.

Once the faces are presented, the bead will squeeze towards the edges and the swirl will secure the inner area without wastage of glue. Have a weight close by to make sure the section dries flat. Here a useful O gauge resin pipe load was used as a wide, heavy block. Books or other flat weights can be used. Ensure that any glue that escapes will not spoil anything you place on top, either by cleaning or using a scrap paper barrier.

*Above left*: Construction of hidden supporting pieces for the arches. A steel weight is being used to secure the pieces until the glue cures.

*Above right*: Pre-built major components ready for detailed sectional assembly.

*Below left*: Arch construction from the major subcomponent sets.

*Below right*: Dry-run assembly prior to final gluing to the platform surface. The useful extra spare sets of print board are being used on the recurve of the wall.

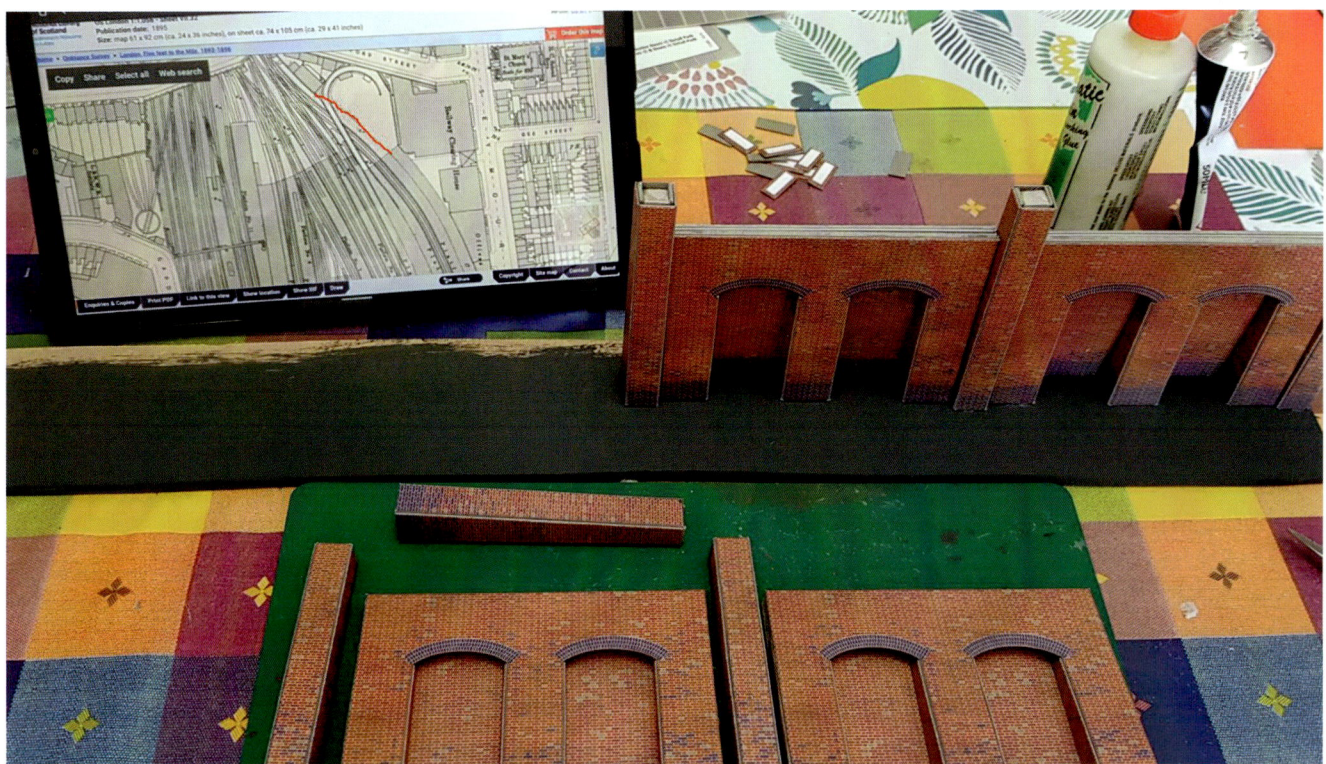

The final gluing of the assembly based on the prototype mapping, using aliphatic resin and clear glue. Here the tablet is showing the outline from internet sourced materials, using the website maps.nls.uk, at which useful historic surveys can be studied. The red line on the tablet screen marks the platform 1 wall line being created at the rear of the RCH facility. If producing something based on a real-life example, accurate mapping is the best start point. The real world can then be simplified and skewed to the available space of your baseboard.

## Supporting Larger Structures

Although the majority of card kits include internal bracing and thicker wall areas, it is still possible over time that they will warp and twist as the material ages and is subjected to heat and cold, dry and damp.

A small kit has walls and roofing of insufficient span to have a large effect. However the flagship products of large railway and bus stations, parish churches, factories and mills have much longer flat walls. Small deviations due to material ageing over time will show up.

At our Club a balsa wood bracing is favoured. Balsa is a lightweight and stable material. It is relatively inexpensive and can be purchased in square rod or sheet form and easily cut to size. PVA or clear glues will adhere it to the inner surfaces of a card building. Alternatively, you can pre-make your own 'L' beams from the stiff scrap card of the kit fretwork, and cut to size as required.

# 4
# Plastic Kits

Plastic kits of railway infrastructure and general buildings are a great way to introduce 3D surfaces to your layout. Often embossed with brick finishes, and containing window frames and metal details, they present a fast and affordable method of populating the scenery. Steel girders, which appear frequently on railway infrastructure, are a prime example of the benefits of these, imparting a good structural shadow. Here, sitting in Dorking Town sidings on Gane A bogie bolsters with Lowmac match trucks, is the Braithwaite steelwork for new overbridge number 1253. This is to allow for a widened A24 at Dorking Deepdene station. Pictured on 9 May 1964. (*AND-M516-1 Online Transport Archive*)

## An Industrial Building for North Cape, Kimberley

The Wills range was purchased by Peco in 1998 and production moved to their Devon manufactory. Our example of an industrial building (convertible to a supermarket) had been stored by ourselves for a while and some parts had donated themselves or been lost on the way. So this represents a typical situation that many modellers go through with plastic examples, where parts find their way onto other layouts, dioramas, or just get lost or broken. The small industrial building genre often sits adjacent to rail routes, sometimes built in redundant goods facilities or as infill to existing unplanned growth.

It helps to look at real examples to get the feel for them, either as single units or based on an industrial estate. They require fencing, security, lighting, places for employees and customers to park and a reason for existence. Thinking up your industry, giving it a corporate colour and logo of your own design, planning and designing the surroundings, all add to the fun of the build and also the realism at the end of it all.

This kit is destined for the Club's South African Layout based on the Grand Karoo semi-desert towards Kimberley. Often forgotten on layouts are the less pretty aspects that accompany the railway into an urban area, such as sewage works, distribution companies and light industry. This building will form the hub of a small industrial estate prior to the station platforms with the aim of imparting a feel of realism as the wild gives way to human influence.

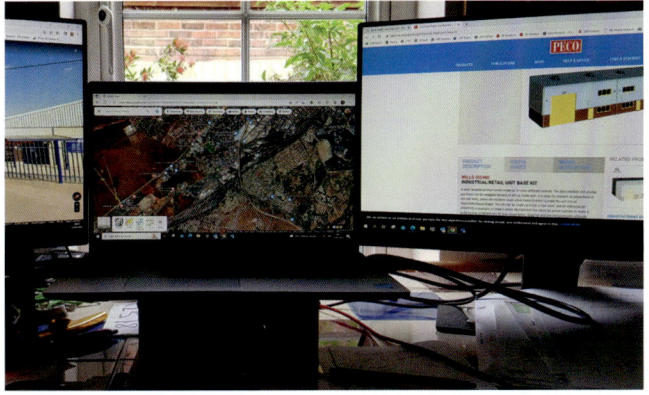

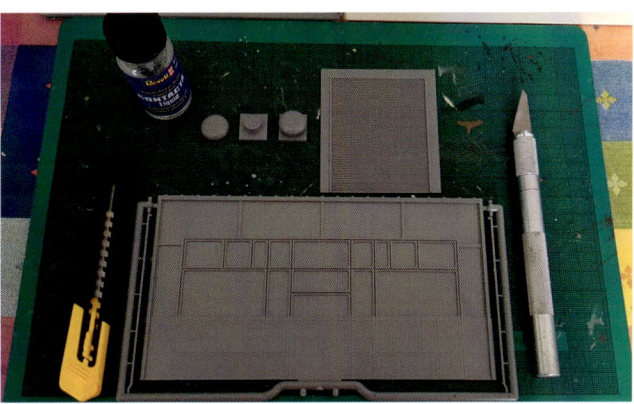

*Above left*: On the right, the manufacturer's image of our target. A typical steel-framed building for light industrial use appearing next to rail lines worldwide since the 1970s. The Club requirement was for a low relief model with some added detail in order to fit the urban outskirts of our South African North Cape, Kimberley layout. *(Image: Peco)*

*Above right*: The kit basics; testing for flatness of the major panels. When preparing plastic kits with larger flat components, it is always important to let them 'rest' flat in a warm room. When stored they can be exposed to heat or pressure, making them warp slightly. If needed, subject them to a heavy book or similar spread weight overnight to ensure they start flat. In extremis, use hot water or a gentle warmth from a hair dryer. Here a liquid 'poly' glue is to be used for most seams and a general gel adhesive for areas that need greater strength over time. You can use these in combination: the quick glue of the liquid in order to build, followed by a seam of the gel glue to strengthen when set.

*Below left*: Preparing corners for cut-outs. This kit has multiple guides for different cut-outs according to the type of building to be constructed. A pointed blade is used here to pierce the corners and ensure a sharp delineation, plus this can avoid an accidental cut or tear into the surrounding material. Be careful when blade-cutting plastics – the cut can run away off-direction or towards the modeller as the blade 'self lubricates' through the soft plastic.

*Below right*: Two long cuts have been made right through the material on cut lines that come off the base of the walls. Here the cutting overshoot just hits the cutting mat. The top cut has scored approximately halfway through from the rear. Subsequently bending the soft plastic as a 'hinge' shows the line on which a front face score will free the material without damage to the remaining wall face. If you were doing this to an older, stored kit the results would be variable, because over time the plastic loses oils and becomes brittle, harder to score and cuts will snap rather than bend. We use a mini drill with a rotary cutting disc for these.

Trimming and filing where a cut line has wiggled a bit, or you need a revetment of some sort, as seen here. You can trim by taking slow pull cuts using a long knife blade. This is where the snap-off blade knives come in useful. You can overextend and use them in a gentle sawing motion to remove spoil. Once filed down, a small warding (or locksmith's) file can then be used to finish off the edge. Alternatively use an emery board or some fine grade sand paper wrapped around an ice lolly stick and gently draw along the edge.

 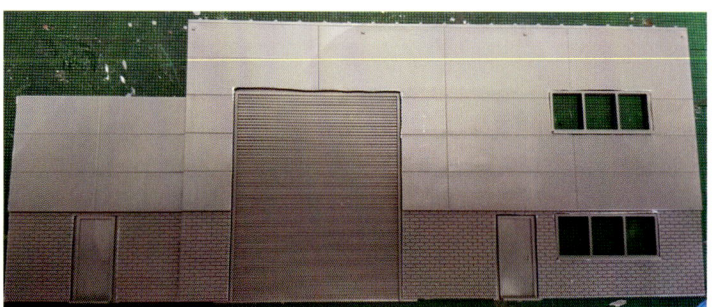

*Above left and above right*: The section removed for the roller shutter door is a large enough offcut to create a reception extension on the side of the main structure. At this point the orientation is important as related to the use of the building. For example, if a tyre fitter/supplier, then reception would be on the left next to the vehicle access as show in the image. If a supplies company, the showroom/reception would be central, with deliveries made to the roller shutter door. For this example we have a light engineering company. Reception will be as far from noise sources as possible and therefore the extension will be on the right, as will visitor parking bays. Justification for buildings, their use and access, when planned properly, will draw the eye to the familiar and make a layout feel correct.

Undercoating components. These kits have a good satin finish on external plastic surfaces as well as a decent brick definition. As a result, since there hasn't been much handling they have not been cleaned. Grease marks from hands or production/packing will prevent good paint adherence, so if on inspection there is contamination, clean lightly with soapy water. Do not use thinners or alcohol. Major components are separated, and edges filed if rough. Smaller accessories are painted on the plastic sprue for ease of handling. Enamels are used here for the brickwork, and later a water-based mortar finish will be applied.

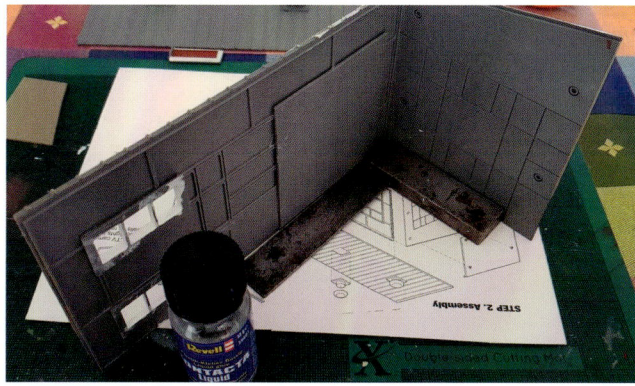

*Above left and above right*: When presenting major wall assemblies together, if you have a 90° angle it will prove a useful asset as parts are glued. Here a pattern-maker's steel square is being used – small and heavy. The vertical seam will be glued using liquid poly cement to secure it by melting bare plastic surfaces in the joint. As a model ages these quick joints become brittle, sometimes even parting after twenty years plus (less if exposed to extremes of heat/cold) due to plastic warping with age. In order to prevent this problem a follow-up bead of clear general adhesive will be run up the inside later.

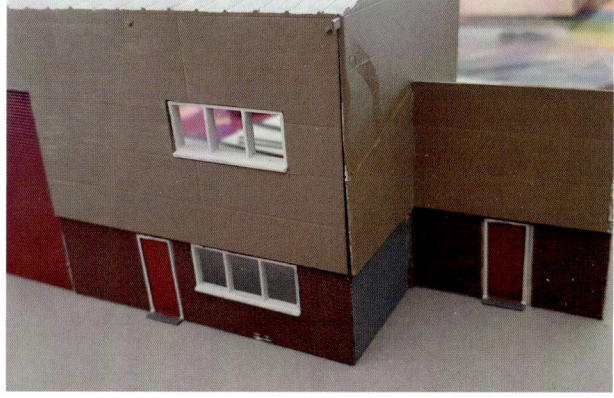

Creating reception. The upper wall surface of the main building has an overlay. A slot has been let into this to receive the new wall addition. Doing this will blend in the extension walls and make the building appear contiguous.

The first topcoat is in place, but corner and seam gaps will have a fillet of lightweight modelling filler to make sure they are seamless in the final model. It is important to blend such elements together or hide them behind a convenient tree or two on the finished layout.

Square section bamboo food skewers are your friends. Here they are being used as inner joints for the reception extension to stabilise edges and guide the roof profile. The untouched skewer will be cut to size and glued into the long section of the large building roof, centrally under the ventilators, rather like an RSJ beam. This is to prevent concave bowing of the roof over time in the completed model.

Corners and seams are infilled using lightweight filler. This 'ever damp' type filler is applied with a small palette knife to force it deep into the gap and a sweep of a finger with a lint free cloth is used to clean off the surface residue. This dries quite hard and can also be sanded if needed, giving a fine powdery residue.

Topcoat applied to upper building and filled corners. A highly watered-down acrylic in mortar colour is added on top of the base enamel of the brickwork. This tones down the dark brick colour and settles in the embossed mortar courses. The same was also used on the roof to pull it back from white and age the 'metalwork' panels.

Smaller detail is added next: drainage downpipes from square rodding, PIR light and IR detectors, important for security, and some company logo additions. Also, panoramic interior photos were sourced online and printed out to form the lit interior details.

The backscenes of the machine shop and office space are glued into place. An LED light will be placed between floors, against the inside wall, to illuminate both floors.

*Right*: Illumination test by flashlight. When placing an interior scene, the depth of field needs to be determined. The closer to the window the better the image clarity. Using a panoramic image gives the opportunity for the viewer to not just see the interior from 90° to the frontage. Normally the view will be top-down onto a layout so you can lose some ceiling, but a perspective floorscape adds to the realism.

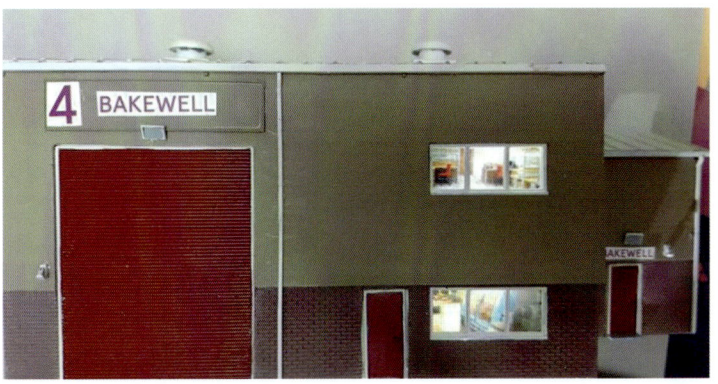

*Below*: Finished and in situ on the industrial estate. Tramway tracks in a concrete roadway, a cola delivery and South African rolling stock complete the scene.

A great thing about some plastic kits is that they can often be repurposed with ease. This is especially true where the kit concerned has features that can be abstracted with reference to a prototype. This example is on the author's O gauge Wroxeter Roman Road layout. There are four plate girder bridge sides over a canal, which are made from Dapol (ex-Airfix) OO locomotive turntable kits. A DJH brass kit of LMS 4-6-0 Royal Scot 6135 *The East Lancashire Regiment* shows a clean set of wheels departing with a five-coach Chester-bound lunchtime service portrayed as in 1947.

# 5
# Wood, MDF, Resin and Metal Kits

Your own selection of mixed media kits that are best for your purposes from different suppliers will result in interesting railway infrastructure solutions. The Cromford and High Peak Railway was very much an ancient make do and mend affair where water had to be brought in old tenders for use of both man and machine. Seen here at Middleton Top on 20 July 1954 is 2F 0-6-0T 58860. Designed by Park for the North London Railway in the 1880s, it transferred to High Peak in 1931. You can envisage the mix of kits and materials that could be used to duplicate such a scene on a model. (*AND-M206-1 Online Transport Archive*)

## Some Options

- **Laser-cut card.** A stiff card base is enhanced by laser embossed/cut parts. Kits such as this are available from manufacturers such as LCUT Creative. A factory chimney uses this approach in the industrial chapter of this book. Such structures often include laser-scribed brickwork and other detail.
- **Laser-cut MDF (medium density fibreboard).** Utilising a thicker walling these laser-cut kits are a great way of

producing a solid medium-weight construction that is robust and capable of supporting a multitude of external finishes. As laser cutting technology evolves so does the variety of examples available in each scale at a reasonable price point. You can use clear multipurpose glue or wood glue to construct the carcase. The finish can be in embossed plastic/paper, printed paper or, after painting with a coat of PVA glue, plaster can be added for stucco or stonework finishes. At our Club we have great experience with www.petite-properties.com for this type of building.

- **Plaster.** A freelance technique using silicone mould plaster kits was popular in the 1980s in the UK using the Linka system. They were best on fixed layouts as they had a degree of fragility, but the ability to use watercolour, gouache or acrylic finishes on them led to some very realistic examples. Out of production, they are being reproduced now by www.linkaonline.co.uk.
- **Resin kits.** Resin kits are popular with wargamers and a number of very accurate specialist kits exist for the modeller, notably for railway lineside infrastructure. Airfix wargame and other examples can be manipulated, often as expandable panels, to scale up as required for a larger building. They can be solid or made up of components. At the Club we have used examples for UK outline from www.skytrex.com/pages/model-railways, notably with O gauge buildings. For North American examples we have used Hydrocal mouldings from www.downtowndeco.com.
- **Metal kits.** Perhaps seen as an older method of constructing small buildings, kit-building with metal is still popular in American outline scales. You get decent detail, but the end result can be quite weighty.

*Above*: Petite Properties MDF kits used on Market Obthorpe in O (*left*) and Witham in OO (*right*), showing just how finishes, as well as scale, can differ.

*Right*: Skytrex resin station extension with a moulded detail interior. This can take detailing to a new level with comparative ease.

The old Linka system involved the modeller making a stockpile of plaster panels and then gluing them together ready for finishing. These examples are very much a millstone grit Pennine Hills finish.

## An O Gauge MDF Project

The Butterwick board extension included an angled site where a watermill was required next to a small stream and leet. A 'Washtub Cottage' kit from Petite Properties was selected to be trimmed for the site and converted to represent a rundown mill building. There were several requirements decided upon in advance, as follows.

- The waterwheel would be implied but not present to avoid scenic overcrowding.
- Originally thatched, the building would be portrayed with pantiles.
- Some Victorian addition to an earlier building was required to give a patina of age, predating the railway.
- The external plasterwork was to show some wear in places down to the underlying stonework.
- Heavy weathering was required – damp, neglect and destitution.

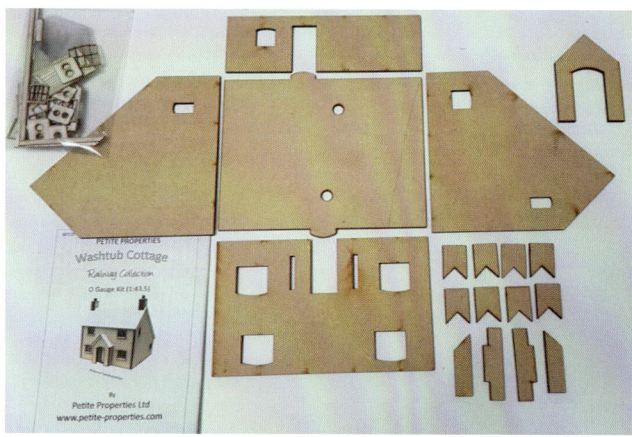

*Above*: The Washtub Cottage kit laid out. It is a combination of heavier laser-cut MDF for the walls and thinner more detailed laser-cut doors, windows and bargeboards.

*Above*: The building frontage was constructed as a free-standing element. At this time the three chimney stacks were assembled for offering up. It is useful to get the mind thinking of logical positioning within a domestic setup.

*Left*: The building needed to abut the backscene at an angle and therefore required a section to be cut out.

# WOOD, MDF, RESIN AND METAL KITS • 37

*Right*: Inhaled MDF dust can be harmful. Therefore cutting with a fine-bladed backsaw was undertaken outside. A small circular saw or fine bladed jigsaw could alternatively be used.

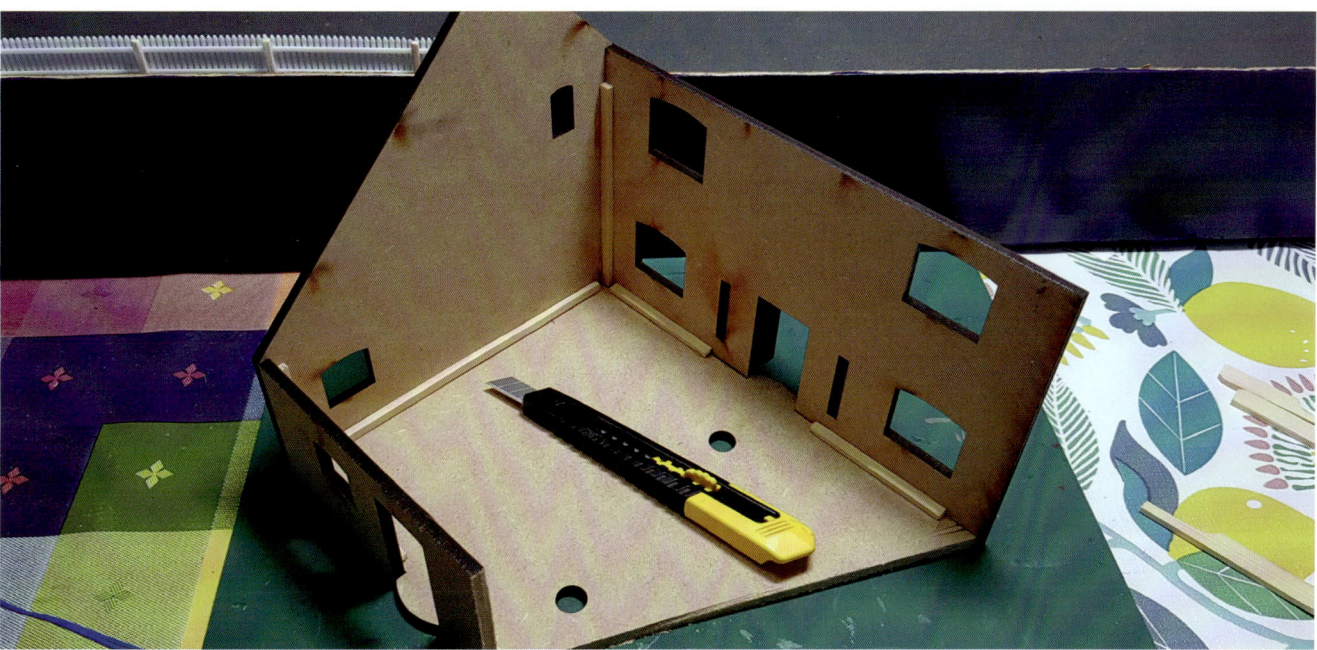

The building is located on a portable board, therefore extra strength was needed for it to withstand transport. All right-angle joints were reinforced by adhering square section bamboo BBQ skewers into place. Others in the Club choose balsa as it is easier to cut.

Foamboard was used as a foundation baseboard. This layer acts as a shock-absorbing buffer should the board be dropped in transit or setup.

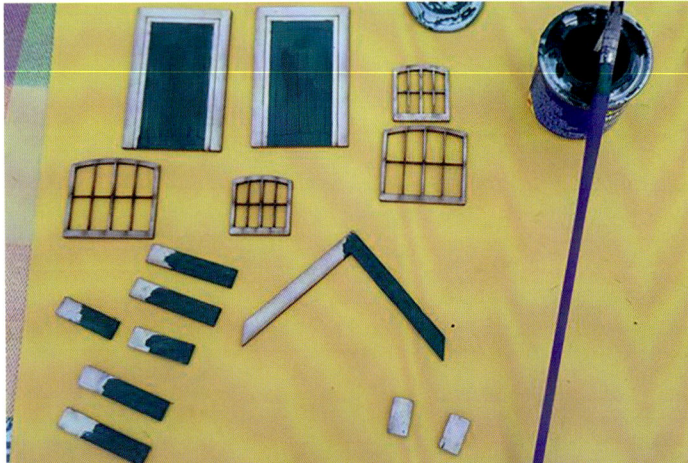

*Above*: PVA wood glue was screeded over the lower surface of the foamboard. The building was offered up, weighted and the foamboard was trimmed before final adhesion to the ply surface.

*Left*: The detailed parts in the accessory pack, such as doors and bargeboards, were painted before applying to the model. It was decided that the laser-cut window frames looked like a weathered peeling paint finish, so these were left alone. These models are very good with the laser-cut accessory inclusions. In days gone you would be independently sourcing these as resin extras.

The run-down feel of the building required gaps in the plaster rendered surface, showing blockwork underneath. The stone colour in these patches is kept in line with the rest of the layout to give themed coordination.

*Right*: A coverage of slightly diluted PVA adhesive was brushed onto the outer faces of the walls. This serves as a keying layer and prevents the following plaster layer from leaching into the contact surface.

*Below*: An oversized 3D-printed industrial window was sourced from the spares box. This was given a brick paper backing to create the Victorian addition to an older building. Saving odds and ends from previous projects is important and can add to the unique properties of your build.

Coarser external filler powder was mixed with water and PVA to plasticise the mix. 'Gloopy' is the best word for the plaster. It has to remain in place without running. An artist's palette knife was used to apply it, leaving gaps for the underlying stonework to come through.

Offered up into place and allowed to harden overnight. Any textures can be added at this point should they be desired, together with scribed blockwork, sags and sills before the finish becomes fully hardened and brittle.

To give a down-at-heel feel, a retro washed-out 'light peach blossom' was selected from the National Trust tester pot range. Using premixed paint examples that real houses would have used over the years is a good way to blend buildings into your chosen time period.

A raid on the pasta jar in the kitchen was called for, in order to secure a supply of spaghetti for the roof. Over this, paper strips were moulded into place using dilute PVA and a broad soft brush to give the effect of pantiles. There are a number of variations on this theme – some choose to use embossed plastic, others individual tiles.

For O gauge, lines of red 80 gr/m2 paper were stuck over the spaghetti to represent the tile courses. When this was done in a OO project, tissue paper was used over vermicelli (a finer pasta).

Working from the scenic backing side of the house, this is the opportunity to add super-detailing if desired. This house has no behind-window detailing. It was deemed far enough back on the layout that interior room details at the viewing angle would be wasted.

Nearly completed, the porch now being worked. As you reach this point it is time to step back from any model. Do you have a colour defined for finishing? Should any plans change? Before fixing the model into final position, you should determine if there are any dead scenic areas. Remember your adult-sized fingers cannot reach some areas, but in your mind's eye you still have that youthful size and agility.

The home run. We chose 3D printing for the roofline, giving some crisp peaks from the strong PLA material. The base acrylic coat of terracotta colour was mixed and laid on quite thickly. Once dry and solid the pantile valleys received 2B pencil lines to delimit the tile joins. Weathering was then applied in a number of different colours to represent moss, lichen, soot, leached lime and guano.

Weathering is fun, but use light touches at all times. It is easier to build up than take off. Have a photo reference of your desired effect. Think where rain will create green moss/lichen trails from window ledges; where shadowing is needed for fallen plaster; where rust from iron/steel windows would be. Don't be afraid to mix up your weathering materials: experiment with dry-brushed card, coloured pencils and weathering powders. For non-absorbent finishes, thinned paints such as enamels, acrylics, oils and watercolours can be very effective. Weathering is an art, so you have the same choice of the panoply of materials regular artists use.

Finally, the scenic blend is done. Your building sits seamlessly into the vignette you have created. It is extremely satisfying when you return to it and think of what you have achieved.

## Examples from Across the Pond

While there have never been that many kits for locomotives in the USA compared to Britain (though there is much modification of ready-to-run models to represent different railroads), there is a wide variety of build and paint your own kits for buildings. The following are examples used

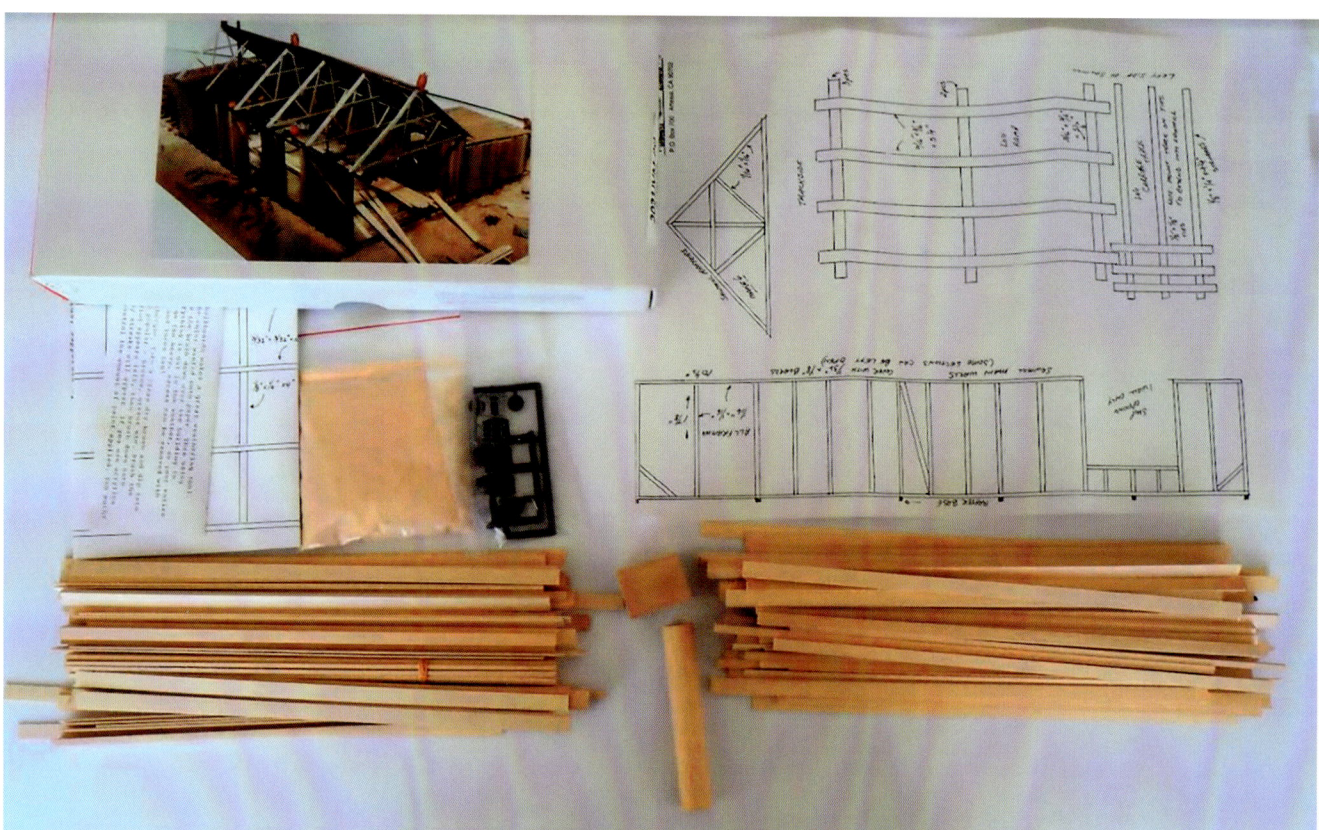

Here is the ultimate kit challenge from the USA. Building a sawmill using traditional 'barn raising' techniques. You can imagine the contractors turning up on site with standard timber lengths. The manufacturer even provides a bag of scale sawdust, which admittedly one would not really be short of when sanding things down. The dowel becomes the basis of a vertical boiler and requires some whittling to adapt. (*Alan Hancock*)

on American outline layouts by Club member Alan Hancock within the sphere of the Club.

Wood stamp or laser-cut kits tend to be highly detailed (as shown in the images of the Mooney's Plumbing kit, the completed green corner shop, O'Lary's Garage, Picorelli's Ice Cream, Buster's Barber Shop). They appear very different from the usual American 'shake the box' plastic kits, such as the Walthers Cornerstone range (though that is excellent). At times they are almost scratch building, because the instructions run along the lines of 'cut supplied wood to the following sizes'. Such kits may include outsourced specialist components such as plastic or multi-layer peel and stick windows, corrugated foil for roofing and metal chimneys. Some suggestions on painting and weathering become mini tutorials in themselves. These kits do however require reinforcing with inner card and a supporting framework. The results can be exquisite, delicate and ultra-realistic. Fos Scale, Campbell, Muir Models, Bar Mills, FSM, JV Models and American Model Builders are among many firms offering wood-based kits. Some of their websites include galleries of models constructed and imaginatively detailed by their purchasers. See You Tuber Jason Jensen who does incredible scenic work using such kits.

Plaster kits are also very realistic and quick to reward the builder when judicious painting and signwriting schemes are applied (Angels Flight Hotel, row of decaying shops). Such kits are not common, and sometimes require 'fettling' to make the parts fit. The walls can look rather thick and heavy (not ideal for portable layouts!) and can crack, *but* the material is brilliant for brick/stone detail because it absorbs colour and you can get very subtle gradation, great for that 'run-down' look. See the Downtown Deco website for examples.

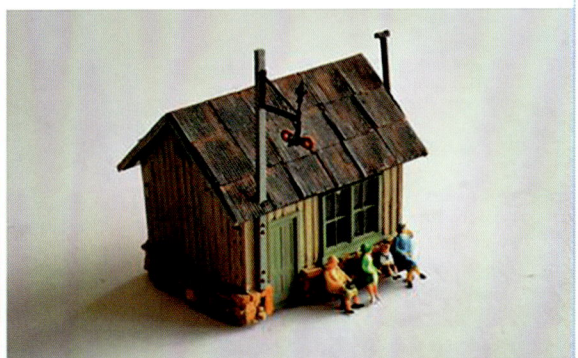

Solid resin (Calletano Clarion by Rusty Rail) and white metal (Guns and Tackle and Block Ice by Woodland Scenics), or mixed media (Station by Chooch Enterprises) can provide much enjoyment in finishing to taste. With white metal a lot of preparation and careful building will be required to produce a decent result.

Solid resin and white metal require special handling. Fine saws and needle files will be required. It is important to ensure the components are detergent washed to remove grease (mould residues). Beware of the dust these products produce – good ventilation and a clean up are essential.

Where there are multiple components and walls to connect, the use of two-pack resin glues (Araldite and similar) is ideal. Rough up the surfaces to be connected with emery cloth. Resin glue provides no initial adherence, so the parts seem to fall apart as if greased. Therefore, combinations of low tack tape, plasticene or Blu Tack and even shuttering style constructions made of Lego and protected by cling film can be used to force parts together until the resin has set and the construction becomes solid.

*Above and below*: Sometimes you just have to sit back, admire and try to work out how to emulate a masterpiece. Seen at the Miniatura 2021 exhibition, this line-up of the Petite Properties MDF laser cut range is called Cobblestone Snicket. These 1:48 scale houses, finished by Rob Crouch Miniatures, are an exemplars of the art form. The chateau has a fully detailed and lit interior which takes a railway model to the level of the best doll's houses.

The interior of the Rob Crouch Miniatures chateau. It shows what level of detail can be attained to complement the detailed shell of a building in these larger scales. It is tempting to make something well to the foreground on a model railway layout, where the view through a window is like a seeing into a real room.

# 6
# Freestyle and Scratch Building

Here on 14 April 1950, BR (SR) Class M7 0-4-4T 30057 accelerates a local service from Poole Station and over the High Street crossing heading towards Parkstone. The railway here slices through an irregular street pattern with Victorian infill encroaching as orchards and gardens were replaced by smaller dwellings crammed awkwardly up to the lineside. Scratch building enables you to create unique constructions to represent the railway cutting a swathe through the pre-existing road pattern of towns and villages. Don't forget the promotional posters and timetables on your layout – in real life if it didn't move it had a hoarding. The signal box here is an exemplar of that habit. (*Online Transport Archive AND-M3-1*)

## Scenic Flat in O: The St Ney Works at Eyton

Occasionally you have the odd-shaped corner or area of backscene where you desire detail but you cannot find a kit that is suitable. In this case the requirement was for a mid-line station halt area on a garden railway with viaducts feeding in. The remit was that it had to be freestyle industrial, appear 3D in minimum depth and be damp and animal resistant.

Choosing a material is a difficult one. In an outdoor unheated location the damp can be a challenge, especially in humid winter conditions. The natural response would be to use embossed plastics or MDF for brickwork, but that would be out of keeping with other parts of the layout which are brick paper wrapped. They can also get beaded condensation on painted surfaces due to residual material warmth when it is foggy.

Good quality corrugated cardboard was chosen (the type that has a shiny printed side, such as pet food sachet packaging). It has a tendency to warp over time but is designed to have a degree of damp resistance and stiffness/strength. When assembly is taking place, alternate layers are at 90° to each other, in the same way that plywood has an alternated direction of wood grain on each layer to induce strength. It was also backed onto plywood for overall module stability.

The space available was appropriate for the concept of a generic factory that was end-on on to the railway, with 'northlights' – the clerestory design used in engineering works which was so popular when artificial lighting was poor.

Factory windows were CAD designed and 3D-printed but this was only from having equipment available from other projects. You can also choose from a wide variety of casements online. Fun was also had with sourcing photographic images of old factories online and printing these out to go behind the windows to give a feeling of depth.

After assembly the finished works was sprayed with a layer of matt varnish. In a garden environment, baby snails have a habit of consuming the paper side of cardboard and destroying the finish – they get in when small and grow as they consume! This easy treatment has been proven to prevent this activity.

The general components of this construction. Upper is the factory walling, slightly offset on the right-hand sides to give a feeling of depth. Underneath is a wooden batten at the represented wall height, giving the factory an elevated foundation. Against this were to be a concrete signalling wire conduit and control boxes, also 3D-printed. Avoid using scissors as they bend the corrugated card. Here a radial cutter was used, but a sharp craft knife on a cutting board will work just as well. Brickwork was image sourced online and then colour- and size-adjusted to the desired appearance when printed.

# FREESTYLE AND SCRATCH BUILDING • 49

*Above*: Construction onto the plywood stiffener was straightforward. You can see the vertical battens to offset the four end walls – they run to full roof peak to discourage warping. This also enabled the underlying factory interior images to offset behind the windows, giving a feel of real depth as the eye moves.

*Right*: Outline completion in an unheated shed on the author's outdoor layout. At this point other projects called, and winter intervened before final detailing and a coat of protective varnish could be applied.

*Below*: Lesson learned the hard way six months later. Baby snails managed to get in through the cat-flap style rail entrance to the shed and teamed up with an early season wasps' nest. The plastic parts could be salvaged and reused but the initial drop in personal morale could have been avoided. Always be aware of where your model will end up, and ensure it can be protected.

## The Railway Clearing House at Euston Station

A wonderful array of detailed pre-builds and kits exist on the market, covering a wide variety of prototypes and eras. However you may require a specific prototype that cannot be sourced, and following research, planning and scaling the decision could be reached to construct your own edifice.

This is true of most of the 1875 Euston diorama being built by the Club. A variety of constructional methods have been used, from a robust but heavy traditional wood and hardboard carcase through to lighter weight, more modern materials. The construction of the Railway Clearing House, or RCH, represents a modular build in lightweight format to allow for easier transportation of a larger scenic section.

Important for any build is the research phase. Using a combination of source books, aerial photographs, maps and plans, the building took form on paper. Gathering a background history added functional clues as to the hidden parts of the structure.

Next is the need for compromise. How much detail, what technique to utilise to physically construct and how large a footprint will be consumed? Then offer this up to the available space and start trimming. What can be reduced, exaggerated or dropped while retaining the overall feel of the building? Giving a sensible feeling of form and function to a visiting public, a club also has to be cognisant that they are attempting to get as close as practicable to the prototype.

The card kit retaining wall from an earlier chapter forms the break between the station platforms and this outside building. A skew to the real life mapped orientation was required to fit to the baseboard plan. Foamboard construction was chosen as foamboard is robust and easy to cut into complex forms. In common with most of the diorama, it was to be skinned with brick papers and 3D-printed windows and doors.

The RCH itself was established in 1848 and using manual collation and filing techniques the staff performed an administrative task that is today extensively computerised. Receiving passenger ticket stubs collected on platforms

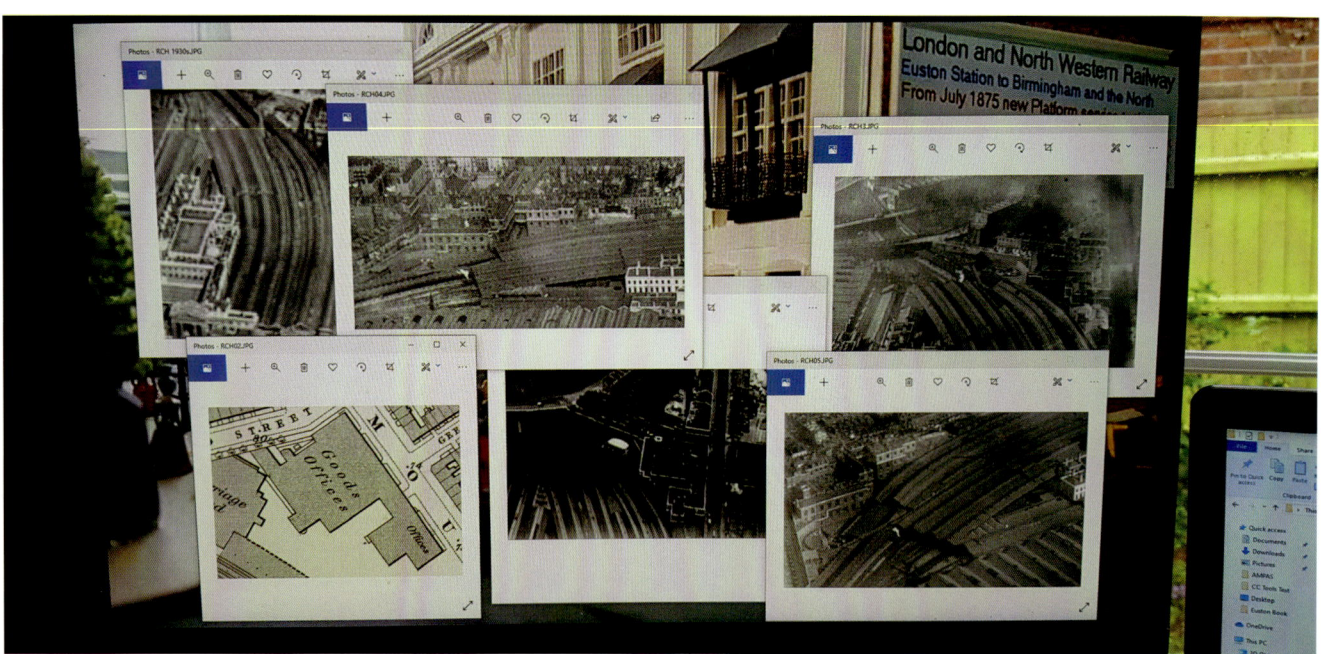

Making the most of modern media. With images collated for personal research on the internet, digitised images from books, maps, even Luftwaffe bombing obliques from 1940, you can get an idea of a building that is no longer present. Fortunately, today Eversholt Street has a line of similar facings from the later expansion of the RCH, so don't rule out Google Street View or a physical visit to a site to get the feel for your target. In his teens the author would occasionally trainspot from a Barnaby Street vantage point, not knowing that one day it would be of deeper interest. Alas the 1978 Ian Allan *ABC* attests that electric traction was never as atmospheric as a roaring Deltic performing its swansong, just down the Euston Road at King's Cross or a Class 45 Peak sputtering out from St Pancras.

nationwide and the counterfoils for freight and parcels portage, the takings from all affiliated railway companies were netted and the charge or payment applied daily to attribute the cost and profit fairly.

Another part of the business was to decide on standards. For example, box and crate sizes and materials, truck and tanker capacities and weight capabilities with an agreed system of comparability between all examples. This is why the appellation RCH is seen against track diagrams and maps, and specific rolling stock designs throughout Britain.

The RCH was a place for keeping records. Agreements were negotiated for track and junction sharing between competing companies. Board and meeting rooms for arbitration were alongside big-windowed work rooms for the human comptometers and clerks. Initially a four person concern on opening, it became a major Somers Town employer and expanded up Seymour Street (subsequently Eversholt Street), occupying the north-eastern corner of the old Euston Station site. Today the site on the corner of Barnaby Street is a major Post Office depot.

A retaining wall with nothing to retain. The Euston baseboards are flat with no attached scenic other than a platform lower front face. This had to be a removable scenic section. The first task was to work at getting the scenic base up to level behind this wall and provide a firm foundation for the required buildings. Pads were cut from offcuts of the same MDF material as the platform edge. This would ensure that a lighter weight, thin ply sheet could be attached on the level.

The spacing pads were glued using PVA as was the reverse edge of the platform behind the retaining wall. The 4.5mm thick plywood was cut to size and placed on top of these, then weighted down until the glue was dry.

Commercial polystyrene packaging from white goods has reduced greatly over the years. When you receive it, as a railway modeller it is good to retain it as it is high density and robust. It is easy to slice with a kitchen knife and very strong in compression. This combines with being lightweight, so it proves ideal for raising the ground level. You do need to be aware that certain adhesives are not happy bedfellows with expanded polystyrene. Here an external window frame sealant is being used. It has a silicone and rubber base and does not dissolve the polystyrene, while allowing initial positioning movement and gap filling.

After being weighed down for a few hours by the railway picture book collection, the scenic sandwich now has a top ply and is ready for building upon.

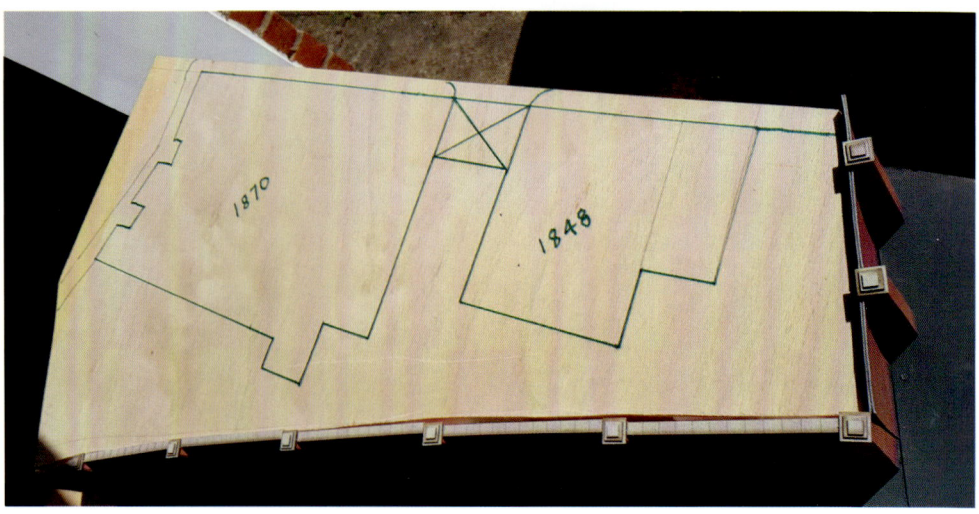

The two buildings mapped out for space. Originally the central horse carriage access had plenty of room for passage round the rear of the buildings, but photographs and maps show that over time extensions reduced this to narrow pinch points. The 1870 building had a central light well between wings which will also be modelled with the glass-topped courtyard roof.

# FREESTYLE AND SCRATCH BUILDING • 53

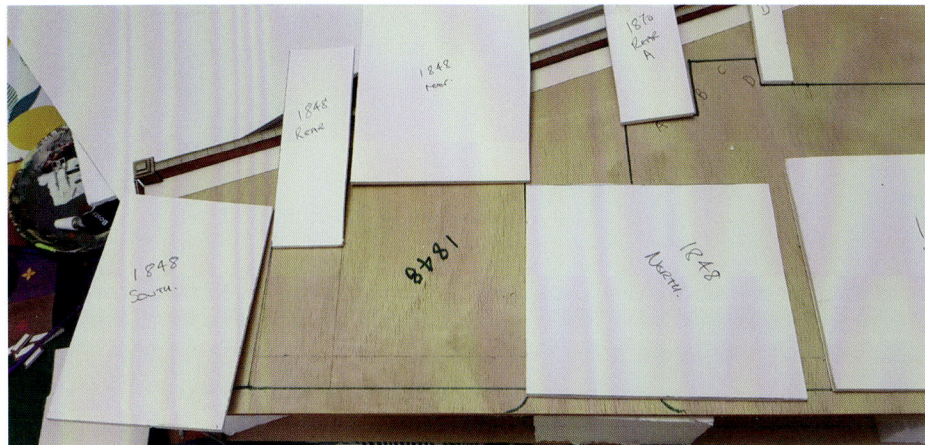

Rough cut of each wall being offered up and labelled before construction. Foamboard can be cut with a sharp knife in situ so post-assembly trimming can be undertaken as required.

Refer to your source material as often as possible – different facets of your chosen building highlight themselves as you progress. Luckily, a 1930s publication called *Railway Wonders of the World* had a section on the RCH including a photograph of the Seymour Street frontage.

Initial shell construction. Foamboard appears to be flat when first using it. Over time, in common with most materials it will react to heat and humidity as well as age, and attempt to warp. Therefore, you also need to plan some internal bracing to prevent this. The bigger the building the heavier the bracing.

The outer shell gets laser-printed brick paper added. A photograph of lightly weathered London stock brick was adjusted and repeated using a graphics tool. Here Bostik glue is being swiftly applied and the paper wrapped around the building. Joints and overlaps of the paper equate to window lines and drainage downpipe positions so will blend in. PVA brushed on could be used as an alternative but makes the paper wetter and more fragile.

An aerial image from 1928 found during the build process revealed that the rear buildings were two storeys. This is where the ability to trim foamboard and brick paper after construction starts is useful. The offcuts were used as bracing pieces to stiffen construction within the buildings.

At this point the frontage resembles the Admiralty Citadel on Horse Guards Parade in London, with a lack of windows and other features. As the 3D-printed extras get added, the repeating pattern of the brickwork paper will disappear. For speed and consistency windows are to be hung as opposed to inset on this building in common with all others existing on the diorama.

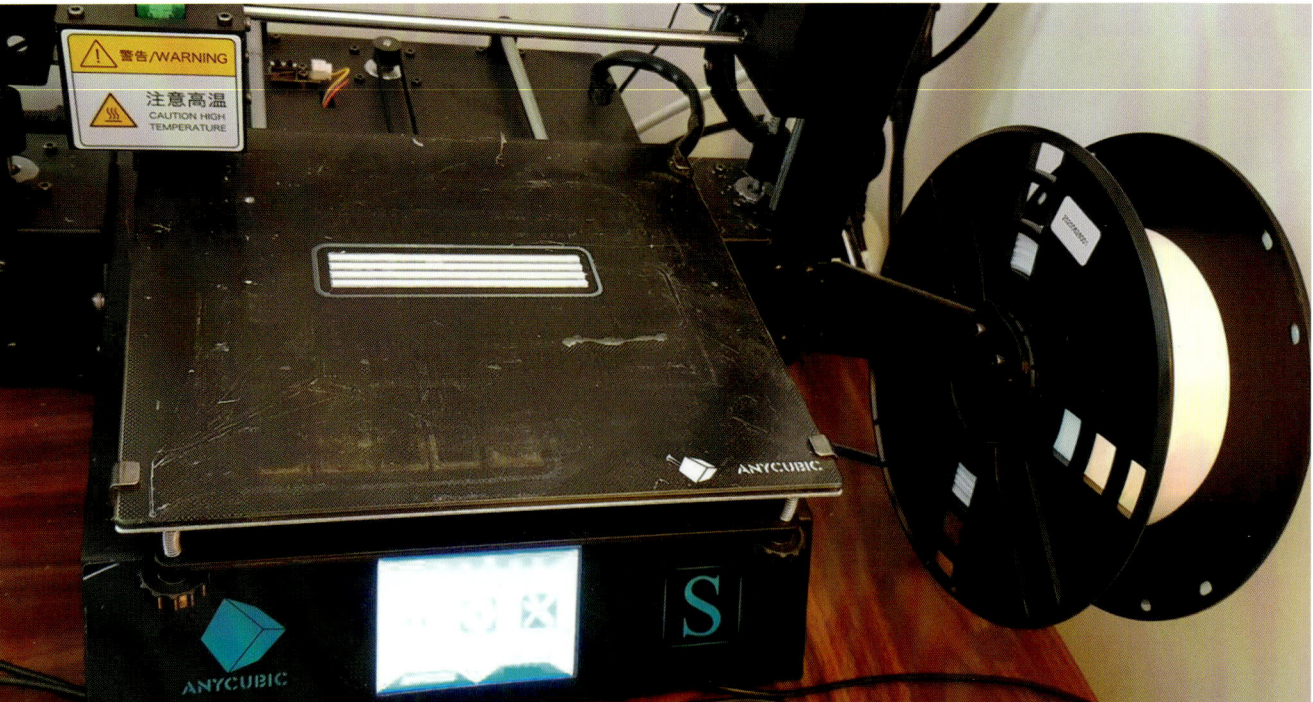

Crown mouldings for the second-floor coursing on the RCH buildings have been 3D-printed. While a seemingly large investment in equipment, a 3D printer can pay for itself in savings on specific detail designs, either as a one off or with repetitive outputs. Model railway clubs are making the jump to invest and take advantage of this technology. Another good reason to consider joining one!

# FREESTYLE AND SCRATCH BUILDING • 55

*Above*: The 3D-printed sash windows and crown mouldings are being collated and constructed ready for addition to the outer surface of the model. Great care must be taken when locating these as any deviation from brick course or vertical drop will show up. Some upper sashes are open; the lower was rarely opened as it would blow documents around.

*Right*: The second floor mouldings are associated with a brick string course proud of the general brickwork, adhered to a card backing, thus creating a 'drop shadow' effect.

*Below left and below right*: Always use a ruler and refer to pre-written definitions of vertical and horizontal positions. Features are being introduced to the 1840 building rear facade. Windows are simply backed by a black marker pen shadow on the brickwork rather than glazed. This is in keeping with the rest of the station model.

Crown mouldings have been 3D-printed for the roof-level wall finish. Rainwater drainage would be behind this with the occasional large cast iron downpipe. The Seymour Street frontage has basement windows behind a protective railing. Here tinfoil is being used as a mirror for these lower windows. Once behind kerbing and railing it will impart a sense of greater depth.

The 1870 building appears to have a light well courtyard in the centre which has a glazed roof to first floor level. The walls are created using brick paper on thin card (the ubiquitous cereal packet as a card donor) and have the windows pre-positioned. Each wall is then dropped into the well as a completed entity and glued into place. This allows for detailing without having to contort oneself in the process. Pet food box corrugated cardboard securely glued and braced forms the basis of the roofing level.

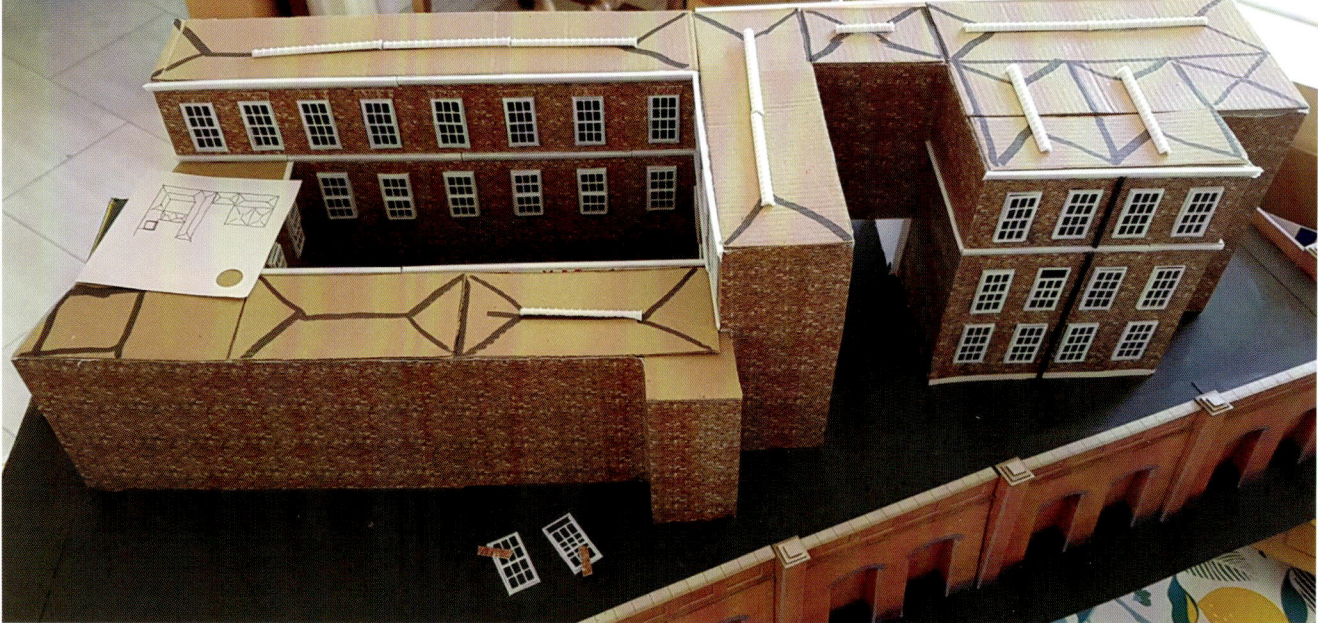

A more cohesive feel to the range of buildings comes when the roof layout begins to be added. Working from plans, photographs and general guided guesswork of the form and function of the building, the roof spaces take shape. Wrought and cast ironwork was beginning to become an innovative building material in early Victorian times (the large spans of work floor in mills and their metal glazing frames for example), but it was expensive. Therefore, traditional techniques were used in the majority of construction where a 'statement' was not being made. Long span timber was being imported to the UK as domestic sources were becoming exhausted, thus challenging budgets. So, the RCH seems to have been constructed with multiple apex roof sections repeated using the shorter softwood timbers and peppered with chimneys despite the apparent provision of a boiler house.

# FREESTYLE AND SCRATCH BUILDING • 57

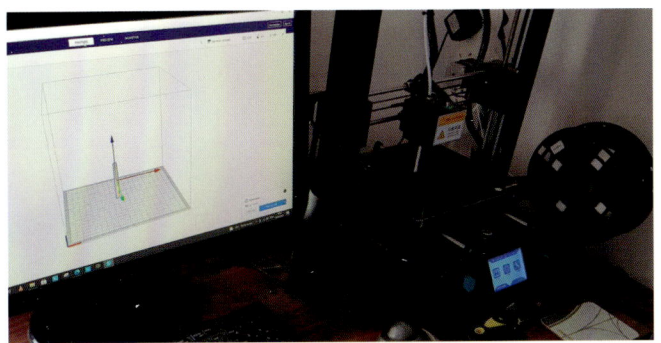

As noted, the advent of 3D printing has been a boon for many clubs and individuals. While there are nicely moulded accessory and finishing parts available off the shelf from companies such as Peco and Slaters, and from the new laser-cutting companies, for the Euston Station models specific prototypes were required and therefore drawn up in a CAD package and printed. Here roofing ridge tiles are printing out.

*Right*: Topping out the model. With larger constructions it is easy to get dispirited. Having personal targets helps. Some tasks are lengthy, others have an immediate effect and rebuild morale. The roofline is a comparatively quick construction and suddenly it looks like a real building. Triangular formers at 45° were made from foamboard then covered in the pet food container corrugated card.

*Below*: Slate effect paper was pasted on using spread PVA white glue. The 3D ridge tiles give a dynamic feeling and the flatness of the slates become visually ignored.

*Right*: At the front of the building we now have two decorative courses, top of window casement bricking and iron railings. The trick of reflecting the basement windows can now be seen.

The view from platform 5 looking east, appearing at this stage like a derelict or bombed out building as the black marker pen window patches are added to the rear offices. With 140 sash windows to be added the decision to surface mount rather than cut in window apertures was felt to be the correct one. It is also in keeping with building reskinning that occurred elsewhere on the layout.

Roof valleys will be lead flashing lined to finish. Because the pitch of a slate roof can only go as low as a 20°, there are two areas that will be flat roofed and leaded as well. It is important to get the roof correct. We don't often see full roof features in real life unless from a high building or in a hilly area, but you always see them when looking at a model railway. Today we can make good use of satellite images and aerial photography to confirm suppositions against the prototype or a similar building type.

The endgame. The testing yard has a 3D-printed 1840s' grounded coach body plus a smattering of containers undergoing standards testing. Below on the long platform 1 of Euston itself a rake of Hornby six-wheel LNWR coaches adds a bit of atmosphere to the view from Ampthill Bridge. Overall, the aim was to present the 'atmosphere' of Euston and not a fully architectural model. At exhibitions the visitor has far too much to absorb and gets the 'shape' of a layout and a lingering memory. The worst critic of a project such as this is usually the original builder. It is always worth stepping away for a while, then coming back with fresh eyes.

# 7
# Lighting Your Buildings

Piccadilly Circus in September 1959 sports a fine array of authentic neon tubing. These were the days when you could actually drive around the statue of Eros, with white-cuffed policemen conducting traffic while on point duty. Lighting is an art form. Even if you do not intend to plunge your layout into 'stygian' gloom there are opportunities to control your ambient light. You can illuminate your streets, and if you wish your buildings as well, in order to generate a feeling of grand theatre. (*Gordon Farrow*)

## The Art of Lighting

In theatrical scenarios lighting is a very important facet and an art form in itself. The model railway is a form of miniature theatre and judicious use of different lighting techniques can enhance the hard work undertaken. You are actually constructing the buildings and then dressing the set. Using a mix and match approach you can 'paint with light' across your model, giving an alternate, naturalistic feel to the crisp light of day that normally invades a layout.

Here we will cover the different techniques involved for external and internal lighting of your model railway as a whole and also the individual buildings.

On the layout itself you may have full control over the lighting depending on the build location. If you have shed, loft or room with blackouts you can combine a full floodlighting of LED daylight wavelengths for maintenance of the layout, and then either dim or switch out to your layout ambient lighting. For those with portable layouts for exhibition, begging a darkened corner will not always be possible. A box-style construction to control external light ingress may be needed to impose shade.

- **Floodlighting.** This gives you less control over the light direction on a layout but can be useful to bring in the overall feel of the location. A desert needs strong whites and yellows, an English summer day greens, the seaside blues and suchlike according to the overall impact desired.
- **Spotlighting.** As with the theatre, if you wish to highlight something consider spotlighting it. To give a real feeling of sun and shadow, a directed light source with a warm hue can be used where all bulbs have the same angle over the layout (as opposed to straight down as is so often seen). As they have a tighter cone they scatter less light and a directional sunlight effect can be achieved.
- **Fresnel effect.** Used often in the theatre but not seen much in the model lighting arena, the concept is to give a softer edged effect by using diffusing lenses in front of the lamp. These can have diffused colour effects, so, for example the running lines get more light and the backscene and frontage get less, You can introduce a gel colour stripe to give the backscene a blue tint, for example. As LED lamps run at a lower physical temperature, the proximity of a diffusing lens will not result in heat distortion or melting.
- **Gobo effect.** This trick is used on some American layouts and is equally at home over here. The concept is to have a strong light source occluded by a sheet with cut-outs. It can be used to give a dappled effect with a green lamp over the top of a woodland area or with a blue/white combination over a harbour or seaside display.
- **Strobe or pulse lighting.** The special effects end of the spectrum should not be forgotten. Your spot welder, base of ashpit glow, bonfire or house fire effects all have a place to highlight a feature, draw the eye and add a feeling of movement.
- **Feature lighting.** Certain features on a layout can be lit day or night, such as the buffer stop lamp, zebra crossing beacons, open or barriered railroad crossings and the occasional emergency vehicle. Be careful though, making things too busy can destroy a scene. LEDs have generally replaced grain of wheat filament bulbs today for accessory lighting. If using a kit normally everything is provided for you. You can also purchase lighting hubs to 'plug-and-play' with groups of lights. Alternatively, if you wish to recycle battery-powered Christmas LEDs or 12V lighting strips you will need to consider protecting them using an in-line resistor. For a handy 'slide rule' see www.evilmadscientist.com/2009/wallet-size-led-resistance-calculator, and for wiring suggestions try www.ledcalculator.net.

An example of a 3D fresnel mask being applied for shadow-inducing moonlight over the Canons Cross layout. This was used for a night-time film scene. Picture a deep box-like grid over the lamp to force an undiffused direct blue/white light over a wide area. This ensures that every object's shadow is the same, and sharp, thus giving the illusion of a true distant sun or moonlight.

# LIGHTING YOUR BUILDINGS

A single LED from a recycled 12V strip being used on a Market Obthorpe shop. The inbound supply is protected by an inline resistor soldered into the red wire. This protects the LED from surge from the accessories transformer as well as ensuring the power presented is within limits, preventing burnout.

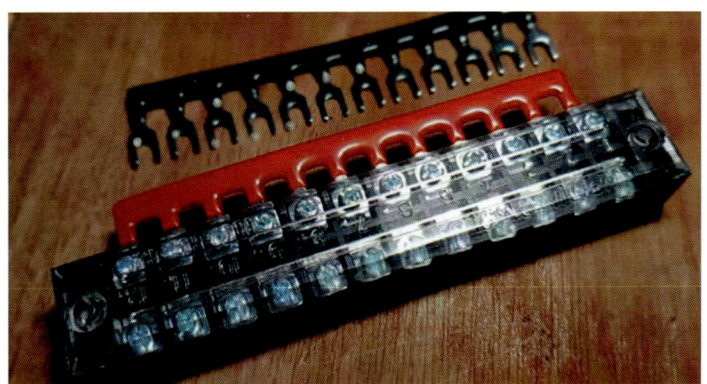

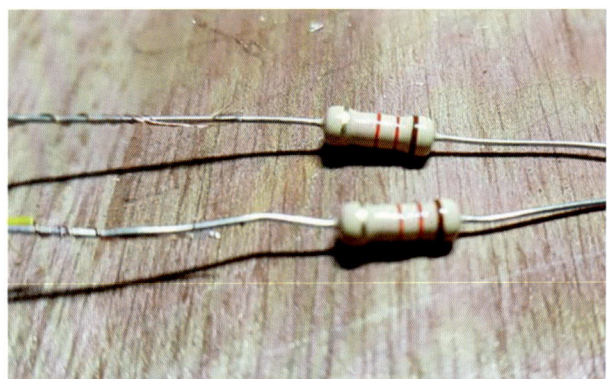

## If Doubt Prevails

If wiring and electrical activities are not your thing, do not panic. Ensure you purchase a kit that already contains a suitable resistor to allow you to use your 12V/16V AC transformer accessory feed. If you connect to the transformer and it smokes, you definitely need a resistor in place (an early personal mishap). It is surprising the number of modellers who buy 12V lights not realising that often more work is required to use them. Some come with a resistor attached inline already, meaning you have no soldering to do. You can use electrical blocks of the screw or clip type to connect to your feed circuit.

If you do need to solder, use a low heat, fine-nibbed modeller's iron. Lighting wires are normally very fine and the solder flows well with a touch and run along the joint. Winding the fine wire around the resistor line works well for a solid soldered joint.

In the Club we work with a common feed and earth return for lighting, taking spurs off to each light in turn. In this manner we are not pushing the strongest power through the first bulb encountered. Each consumes its own potential from the feeder circuit. Some electrical blocks have the busbar option, as shown in the image above left, effectively looping the live/earth feed wires to all the demanding accessories without you creating spaghetti.

If you have just a few lights on your layout, then the accessory feed from a transformer will suffice. However, once you get serious you will find the electrical demand will require a dedicated supply. Club members use separate transformers with 16V AC 1 amp output in a number of scenarios, in some cases using a splitter/rectifier to give sectional controls.

Salthaven Quay in O 16.5 narrow gauge. This freelance layout by Lincolnshire local Stephen Cooper is based on the river Haven at Saltfleet in Lincolnshire and is serviced by the 2ft 6in gauge Lincolnshire Coast Light Railway. It is designed to portray a winter night scene with bare trees and the blue LED night-lighting overall is balanced by warm interior lighting and detailed interiors to buildings to deepen the effect. The colour palette of buildings is limited so that the blue outline light does not clash or alter them substantially. Where cameos are portrayed, they are positioned either under tight beam light sources or outside the larger windows. This gives the ability to 'storyboard' and intimates a greater board depth as the warm light does not mix substantially with the overall blue.

*Above*: The theatrical tricks of good set lighting were revealed to us on our Canons Cross layout. A film production company portrayed it in a cutaway shed as the pivotal prop for their BFI sponsored short film *Dream Big*. Mixing light in colour, intensity, warmth and direction for different shots and emphasis was key to giving the camera technicians their desired shots. None of it was chance, lighting was as pre-scripted as the actual film scenes. While the dangling lights appear rather haphazard and indeed formed part of the set, the light they gave off was shadowless, allowing other effects to be used. You can attempt dedicated effects on a home layout to portray weather, time of day and mood.

*Opposite above*: The construction of this end of the layout is shown later in this book. It represents where most of the action occurred at Thaxted, Suffolk. Canons Cross has street lighting but no interior lighting for the buildings. Most of the time the lack of this is actually not noticeable as display locations normally have diffused ambient light sources.

LIGHTING YOUR BUILDINGS • **63**

Street level, looking uphill on our version of Watling Street in Thaxted. The street lamps appear a little oversize in close up photography. When seen from normal viewing distance oversize is good, as otherwise the eye would lose the actual effect. As they are modern cool LEDs any worries pertaining to the heat of the old grain of wheat bulb technology were alleviated. The lesson is to replace old with new wherever possible.

## Witham in OO by Martin Reynolds

Club member Martin has been building a portable personal layout to supplement Club resources at exhibitions.

Overhead lighting at home can be fully controlled to exclude most light and give a full night-running atmosphere. Accessory power is switched in sections from a control panel by theme, such as yard, engine shed, streetlights and platforms.

Most exhibition venues have diffused flat lighting, meaning displayed layouts to are well lit but lose shadow. The controllability of the domestic setup to allow fuller blackout adds extra atmosphere to these photographs.

Different colour LEDs are used to highlight features. Street lamps have the warm yellow spectrum; diesel depot blue white for fluorescent tubes; and buffer stops with red warning lights.

*Top, above and left*: Canons Cross required a burning building effect for film purposes. Three different stages of damage were required. This image shows the fully aflame house. A combination of a flickering fire effect LED plus a small smoke oil generator was used to good effect. It has to be remembered that you don't want to vape too much. The options of burning wood or coal aromas can certainly add another sense of realism to a scene but can also be intrusive.

# LIGHTING YOUR BUILDINGS • 65

The positioning and strength of an in-building light is important. In this case, on the Butterwick layout, the goods shed is required to cast light out of the windows into the yard and under-light the wagons, so two LEDs are needed – one high and far back for windows casting onto the granite setts, and the other at platform height beaming along the track to the doorway.

A workshop scene enlivening the Butterwick O gauge layout. By using an imitation oxyacetylene torch LED (bright white flicker followed by a red dimming light powered from a 6V battery), the interior machine tool details also get highlighted and drawn to the eye. You can buy these LED circuit boards pre-assembled at shows or online and they add another dimension to your layout.

Don't forget your rolling stock can also contribute. LED lighting can be battery powered (activated by micro or magnetic switches) or direct from a transformer supply such as here. The Butterwick terminus platform has a locomotive isolating section allowing the transformer to remain on and therefore keep the carriage lighting when stationary, contributing to a night scene. If you use DCC, you can accessorise and designate a chip setting for the lighting without the need for such wiring.

# 8
# Railway Buildings

*Above*: Many modellers concentrate their detail purely on the rail-side. Lavishing some detail on the station frontage also adds to your model. Seen on 23 September 1969, the simply named 'City Station' is in St Albans. It holds a wealth of detail in what could be regarded as a mundane shot. The taxi and bus drivers' rest room was built under the circulation canopy of the station frontage with a raw wood finish, destroying the grace of the original building. There are strikes and unrest on the WH Smith news-boards behind the Triumph 2000 saloon. Next to a No Parking sign, a chalked message proclaims that apparently Greg loves Jane Draper! Graffiti on railway property is always an interesting modelling addition but not often seen. Create your own miniature Banksy. (*BRB Derby*)

*Opposite above*: End-of-shed view towards graffiti in abundance on modern image Burnroyds in OO. While the maintenance area is clean and compartmentalised, the railway itself is down at heel. A reversal of the old days when the steam shed was the rust and dirt area, and the six-foot way was maintained with dedication.

*Right and below*: There are times when the railway infrastructure itself carries the scene. Here the Club EM gauge layout Woodcroft displays a rural idyll. The only overt construction here is the bridge and retaining walls over the river prior to plunging into a steep cutting. There is often the desire to cram everything you own or wish for into a layout. Remember that open spaces around your line can also be an asset and serve to emphasise your other buildings. An option is to use a modular approach where you swap out key buildings seamlessly in order to manipulate the character of the model. Butterwick does this to switch between 1962 steam and 1972 pre-TOPS rail blue.

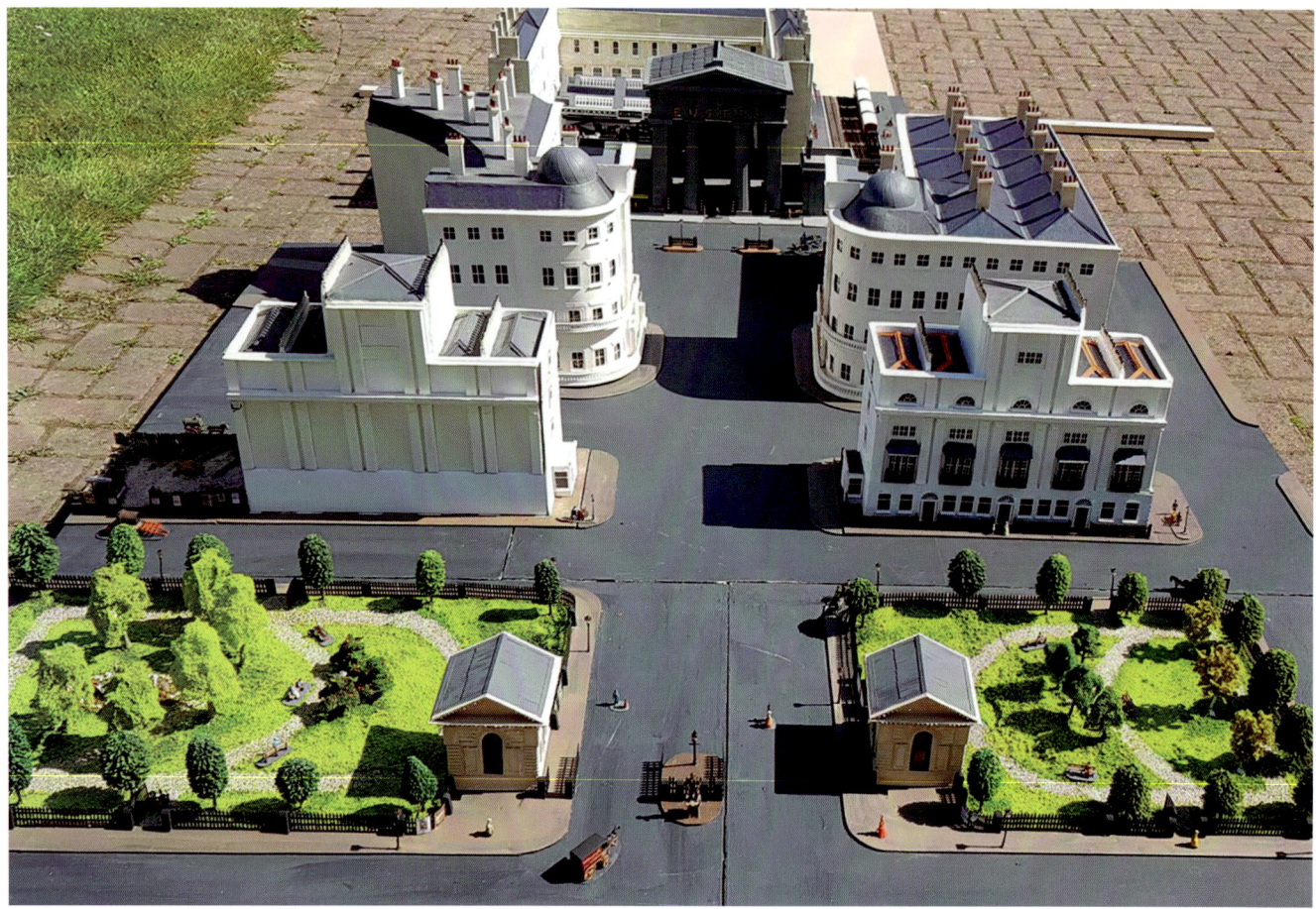

*Above*: The opposite extreme: the Club Euston Station in OO scale. The railway buildings themselves could dominate, however, including foreground Georgian/Victorian parks, hotels and houses is a form of grounding for the model, rewarding the viewer with some grand vistas. It has a historical landscape to entertain the eye which would otherwise be washed away in a sea of cramped platforms and offices.

*Below*: The Club OO layout Deeping Lane MPD has a grand scratch-built coaling facility dominating the skyline. While the 'Western' retained manual loading using small coal tubs to favour the softer Welsh steam coals, other lines were able to take advantage of mechanisation. At the close of steam some of these concrete monsters required explosive demolition to remove.

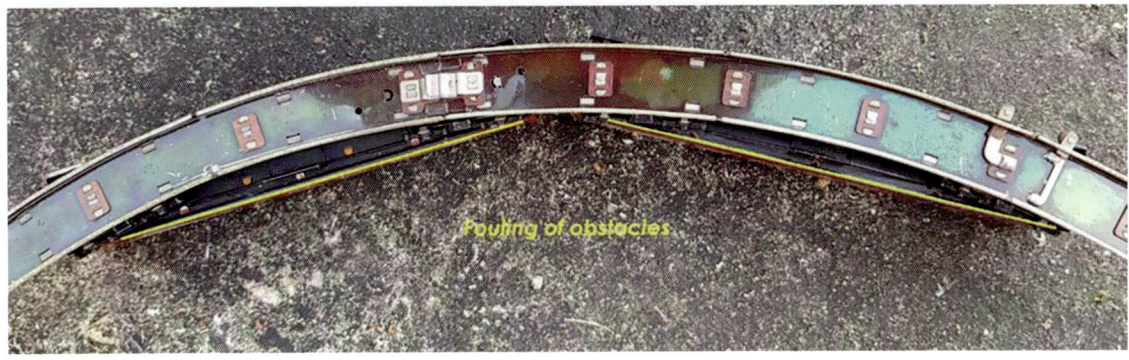

Most layouts will have a station of some sort to bring variety into the running experience. While it is possible to make use of standard prefabricated units, it may not be desirable due to adherence to prototype, baseboard configuration constraints or just the desire to do something different. Height above rail can vary a little without too much of a problem other than perhaps troubling the eye at times, but clearance of platform edge to the rolling stock is as essential in the model as in the 1:1 real world. There are several things you need to check. If you have tight radius curves then you will have issues with overhangs and gaps, especially with bogie stock. If you have turnouts allowing stock into a platform edge, the unrealistic throw of most models will result in them striking the platform. The same holds true with any lineside construction or accessory. Maybe not as pronounced today as it was with the Hornby Dublo example here, but care is still required. Take your longest bogie vehicle, the locomotive with the largest frontal throw on a curve, and a brake van or four/six-wheel coach with lower steps and constantly measure and test during construction.

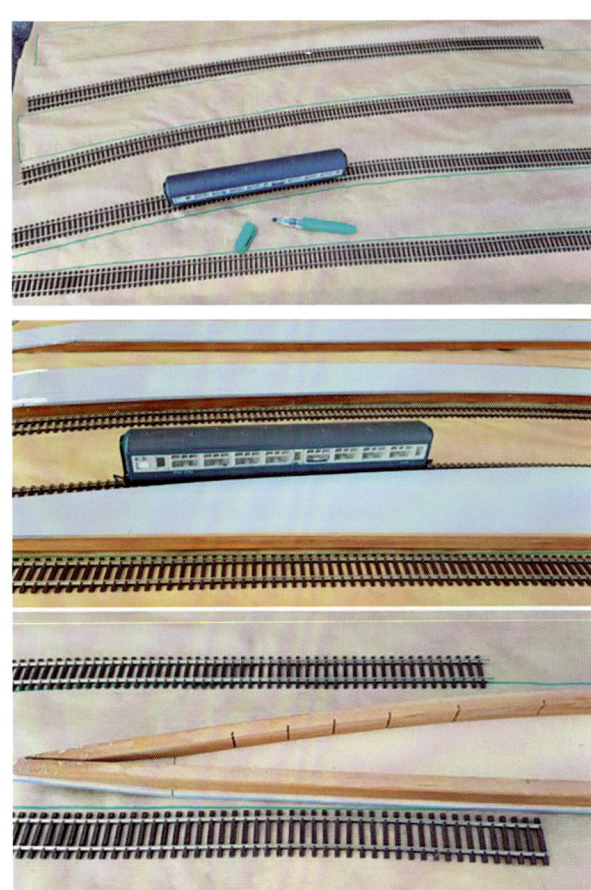

Here is an example of prototyping for a complex station setup before fixing the track. Use wallpaper roll or similar to get your schematic drawing into place. The line geometry is drawn based on plans, aided by flexible French curves (or indeed a spare plastic curtain rail) to give a constant curve where required with flexitrack. Once this is in the desired place, get the rolling stock and a soft pencil (we used a pen for photographic reasons). Place the pencil against the vehicles at the midpoint and gently push around where platforms are required. The variation of lines between carriages, locomotives and outsize trucks can be worked with to ensure you have running clearance for all (picture the blue spot GWR King class with restricted route availability due to outsize cylinders). At the end you can cut out your template of the platform and apply it to the material of the model for cutting and trimming. You can see here a trick used when bending a wooden bead round a bend – interior cut-outs allow smooth bending without any need to steam the wood. Avoid fixing either track or platform into place permanently at this juncture, you will have an easier time as you can jiggle both platform and trackbed to get millimetre-perfect, then glue both down.

Don't forget the homes of those lineside 'deities', the linesman and platelayer's huts. Accompanied by ballast bins and other six-foot way maintenance requisites they can balance out the scenic feel of a layout.

Bridges great and small add to your layout. The example here on Butterwick was 3D-printed from a rescaled model of a seaside pier. This allows the millstream to exit under the station platform.

Viaducts made from wood, plastic or in this case a Metcalfe card kit, can be very robust yet add a feeling of delicacy and interest to your layout.

If you can bring in a rail-over-road bridge, you can narrow your perspective and frame a scene. Here on the Little Salkeld layout of Paul Moss, the Eden Valley stretches away in N gauge finescale.

Club president Colin Brown started coarse scale O gauge railway modelling in the early 1950s, a certain Herr Goering having destroyed his tinplate Hornby in the previous decade. His familiarity with the steam railway infrastructure shines through with Nenthead, his shed and garden layout. Here, Thompson B1 Antelope class 4-6-0 8306 *Bongo* approaches the station past the headshunt. (*Paul Bason*/Railway Modeller)

LNER 0-4-4T G5 class #387 stands at the platform face with a single ancient clerestory coach. The station behind is simple, robust and unadorned reflecting North-Eastern branch practicality. (*Paul Bason*/Railway Modeller)

GE Class T26 2-4-0 runs out of Nenthead station with a two-coach consist to Garagill and Alston. A Raven Q6 0-8-0 shunts the yard. It all feels well proportioned and in line with the prototype. Railway infrastructure details can be many and varied; getting the right proportion and position is the trick rather than overloading the scene. (*Paul Bason*/Railway Modeller)

A medium-sized corrugated iron waiting shelter portrayed at Butterwick station in O gauge. A tip for baseboard joints on layouts that are portable: for platforms, grassed areas and roads always try to carry the material being used as a surface down an overlap on both sides of the join (see far left of the picture). Paint all else matt black. When the baseboard is cramped together, as there is not an abrupt demarcation, the join line disappears.

*Above*: Lollington box on Graham Hobbs's Geatford Crossing layout where the quad East Coast Main Line ends. Open spaces, plenty of room for the signal posts – no restricted clearance markers required for the permanent way team here.

*Below*: Compare the previous image to the cramped commuter-land shown on the Club's Cannons Cross layout. The third rail here adds to the chaotic feel, but the tolerances on everything are good – no fouling occurs even when the long electric carriages come in.

Finally, as rail-side is often viewer foreground, you have the opportunity to get your teeth into interior details. Here is O gauge Market Obthorpe signal box under construction, including a brass detailed interior from Severn Models.

# 9
# Rural Buildings

*Above*: Some rural splendour on the North Downs. Maunsel Mogul N class 2-6-0 31867 making light work of a Saturday up goods at Dorking Town on 7 August 1954. This locomotive overran signals while pulling a parcels train through Gloucester Road Junction in Croydon just four years later, hitting an EMU and injuring nine people in the process. It is perfectly correct to model a station in the middle of nowhere – the railway line was a 'best fit' but often missed the villages on its route by miles, with stations being given a joint name or being called 'something'-road station. (*Online Transport Archive AND-M208-1*)

*Overleaf*: There is a certain grandeur in the decaying abandonment of agricultural buildings. The example here is a small Lincolnshire farm built on the site of a Knights Templar preceptory. If you can give your own buildings a backstory (from fact or otherwise) you often find that the design and execution is improved as you apply reasoning. Buildings decay in a predictable manner. Outbuildings get overgrown quite quickly, damp sets in on woodwork and storms unseat the slates or tiles, leaving gaps. The roofline will subsequently collapse inwards and often take a wall out with it. Domestic premises take longer to fail (assuming no fire or vandalism). Once there is no internal heating the window woodwork and ceiling/roof joists will start to suffer. Glass will slowly be lost but because of internal supporting walls the roof tends to last longer in situ as do the outer walls. The farmhouse here has three different building phases. Reclamation of clerical buildings with walls several feet thick forms the lower layer. The extension upwards is a Georgian phase and the rendered rearward appears to be late Victorian. These photographs are teasers for The Priory, our N gauge layout extension, detailed in an upcoming book of this series and discussed a little later in this book.

*Right*: When it comes to stripping away the construction of a building for dereliction effect you need to know the underlying structure. Seen here in constructional view format is Frindsbury Manor barn by the talented Ken Bonham.

*Below*: Four views of the Greatford Crossing layout rural sections as built by Graham Hobbs. This garden-building based construction is large enough to have a divide between the urban section (Peterborough) on one side and the returning rural tracks through Greatford. The four running lines are accompanied by the crossing keeper's house and very little in the way of rural building otherwise. For impact, if you can avoid cramming your countryside with buildings those that exist will look correct in context. The intimation of farms themselves comes from the fields and grazing animals rather than actual construction of the associated buildings.

*Left*: It is tempting to always portray country stations and their villages as perfect, cared-for entities, but many were on a downward curve towards dereliction by the 1960s. Demonstrating the wrong end of that parabola, motor unit 619 sits against the island platform of Allhallows-on-Sea station on the Hoo Peninsular in Kent, on 19 November 1961. Just a few weeks away from total closure, this branch from Gravesend was suffering from lack of investment and a distinct tourist downturn. (*Online Transport Archive Meredith 486-10*)

## Rural Market Town: The Canons Cross Extension OO

A model railway club sometimes gets requests that are out of the ordinary, perhaps to attend an exhibition that is not overtly railway oriented or to lend some asset as an exhibit. In this case a professional film company approached us as they were making a short film in which a model railway would be the star.

The challenge was that some elements of the layout were required to represent a physical filming location. General building styles, wall colour sequences and roofing types needed mapping to form a curving townscape with a church as the focus to one side. Behind them a brick-based windmill and a single storey thatched cottage became focus areas for the shooting script. This meant that a new scenic board was required to extend the existing townscape and blend into the new area dedicated towards filming. Where to start? We were keen to repurpose redundant boards and recycle materials. An old N gauge layout had been stripped and was of the correct board dimensions. Next a search through the stores. Old or slightly damaged buildings are never thrown away, they become donors for new projects whenever possible.

*Above*: Having seen and measured Canons Cross, the art director associated with the film produced an oversight plan for the modelling phase. The time available (and Covid-19 lockdown) meant that the opportunity did not exist to make a detailed exact copy of Thaxted. Adhering to the colour sequence of the buildings lining the main road as it went downhill was deemed a minimum. A model village and a martial arts dojo were being built by film production students at the University of Hertfordshire, and the exact positioning of every element was essential.

*Opposite above*: Specific buildings had closer location shots associated with them. A thatched alms house and a windmill were examples of these. The true geographical position could not be portrayed, but they could be repositioned into a vacant rear corner of the townscape.

The alms house made use of a pre-existing two-floored kit. However, we needed a single floor portrayed. Wrapping the lower floor in black duct tape and dropping into the polystyrene substrate used as the landscaping gave a nice tarred damp course effect. The windmill was a licence-free 3D print from www.thingiverse.com. Wrapped in brick paper for speed of creation it became a generic representation close enough to the original for camera cutaways.

# 78 • CONSTRUCTING BUILDINGS FOR MODEL RAILWAYS

Summer 2021 and out of Covid-19 lockdown at last. The team meet to rough out the baseboard for the rural town element and compare to the plans provided. Making use of existing and often damaged pre-built models meant plans also included how to rehabilitate them.

Part of the rural charm of Thaxted is that Watling Street dives down a pronounced hill as it passes the church. Positioning houses so that they had access alleyways and back detail to be picked up on camera was important. There is no backscene obstructing the view. A series of polystyrene plateaus was created to drop the buildings down alongside the road and pavement.

This plastic kit was thought to be a write-off, missing windows and chimney stacks, and painted in a bright red gloss all over. We brought it back from the brink with a coat of PVA coat on top of the red to block any colour bleed. This was followed by silk white enamel to bring it into line with the plans; 3D-printed lettering was then put into place on a signboard.

First integration fit with the materials from the degree course students included on the board. This was a display at the 2021 Miniatura Doll's House and Miniatures Show and proved that a proper scaled drawing of the main building areas was fundamental to success. Buildings along Watling Street were painted by purchasing match pots of the National Trust colour emulsion range, therefore duplicating the real street hues.

## Lessons Learned

Shown here are images of the finished model looking uphill and the real Thaxted Watling Street, so that you can see the liberties taken between model and real life. The majority of models seen here were either recovered from vandal-damaged stock or donated examples. The aim of imparting the general feeling of the town versus an exact model was achieved on a shoestring within the time constraints.

Building on a hill takes some working around but is a great asset. So many townscapes are flat as a pancake but vertical change, while a challenge, gives a good feel to a construction.

When recovering damaged models, if you are unable to strip strong colours, a coat of slightly diluted PVA followed by a neutral undercoat works wonders.

Taking the colours and general feel of buildings works well. You can see where we made use of different styles or joining of buildings, but the use of the colour sequence hid the majority of difference from the prototype.

Ensure that the roofing colour and style of your buildings is generally correct. The majority of the time you are looking down on a layout. The use of slates, tiles, thatch as a consistent theme with the prototype positions your model within a geographical location.

Don't worry. As ever, the originating modellers eye is often far more critical than that of the casual viewer.

# 10
# Urban Buildings

In 1950s London, street markets saw a heyday of activity as warehousing and industry declined. Here is Farringdon Street flea market in November 1956 looking over to Wren's St Bride's church in Fleet Street. The wall fronts onto the railway cutting on what is today Thameslink between St Paul's and Blackfriars. The trams have gone and the Booth's gin distillery is on its way out, but overheads still exist for trolley bus use. We see dowdy clothing, grey everywhere and there is a general feeling of austerity, despite being two years after rationing ended. Don't be afraid to weather your urban buildings as they were quickly polluted and pristine colours diminished. (*Gordon Farrow*)

An earlier urban street market portrayed at the end of one of the Euston Square Georgian terraces in 1875. Despite inherent pollution here the London buildings are comparatively new and bright. You can justify the finish based on the age of the building during the period you portray.

# Urban Excess: Euston and Somers Town in OO

This is the pet project of the author through the Covid-19 lockdowns, taken on after the initial donation of the core diorama to the club.

In addition to the urban sprawl- or market town-style of model, there also is the city centre, built as a statement and normally consuming a lot of space. The Club's Euston layout in 4mm OO scale, and when fully assembled occupies eleven board sections covering 100sq ft (9.2sq m). It is too large for full setup in the clubhouse and protrudes from a standard garage, however it is a good anchor for an exhibition. Despite the size it represents just half the station. Perhaps it is an example where 'think big then reduce' should have been the maxim, or maybe it should have been built in 2mm N scale. Certainly, for a domestic model project it could be deemed excessive, but in an exhibition context or purpose-built shed it can be justified.

The buildings are monumental Georgian and Victorian edifices set in the year 1875. The layout has an exaggerated vertical scale in some areas to pull the eye into false perspective through the layout length which is attenuated when compared to the real station and city buildings. The eye can be fooled in a number of ways in a model, via backscenes and low relief, reducing or increasing scale slightly in different dimensions and the use of tonal colours to give depth. You can read about how this was done by Disneyland – the same can work on your models.

Euston Station seen from the grand southern vista in 1875, a view soon lost when the hotels joined over the roadway. Buildings are wood and hardboard cubes, faced with cereal packet cardboard and 3D-printed detail fittings added later. Rooflines are from cat food boxes. While not using expensive materials, the time and patience involved represents the investment.

When building up an urban area, amenities and parkland are as beneficial to the modelling eye as to the real population of an area. Euston Square Gardens bring green relief to the expanding metropolis.

The view along the now lost section of Drummond Street – a veritable canyon between the Victoria and Euston hotels and the entrance to the station. Build high and get rewards when you dress the set.

Urban areas lend themselves to displaying a grand vignette. Here on the station arrivals platform is the band of the Coldstream Guards and government representatives preparing to greet the Sultan of Zanzibar returning from a northern trade trip.

URBAN BUILDINGS • 83

*Right*: The long view from the RCH (Railway Clearing House) featured earlier in this book, through to the far southern end, anchored on the Euston Road. Only the eastern half of the station is portrayed – common sense prevails.

*Below*: Cutting or slicing the station allowed the building to display its innards. The Euston Great Hall has a diorama viewed through the open western wall, giving the opportunity to show the wonderful architecture. LNWR police clear the public from the east side of the hall ready for the Sultan. Slice a church, a town hall, a swimming pool and display that little extra.

## Urban Lineside: Medehampton in OO

Club member Graham Hobbs has built a highly detailed personal layout based on the end of steam on the East Coast Main Line around Peterborough. It is part open country with four running lines, then it plunges into the seemingly never-ending low-rise, red-brick city.

The core of the City of Peterborough, originally called Medehampsteade, is based on a Roman settlement and the infrastructure is medieval around the cathedral precincts. There is an extensive sprawl of later Victorian suburbs developed around the station, and railway yards and a loco shed up to the brick yards called Hampton. These have all been modelled in exquisite detail.

*Left*: What makes an urban scene? Certainly, major infrastructure such as that shown here with the A47 (now A1179) Crescent Bridge over the East Coast Main Line. Often there is a lack of natural green relief outside parks. A main road and low relief backscene combine to give a feeling of depth.

*Below*: The view from a railway carriage in a built-up area is often one of repetition with detail differences to attract the eye. The back view of terraced or semi-detached Victorian houses changes through the years ( for the fronts, see the photographs of terraced housing in Chapter 3, p. 22). Originally, they would have all have looked seemingly identical, apart from doors and drainpipes in a limited colour palette. Over time tenants or owners imposed their will over the structures, changing them physically, adding extensions and lean-tos for inside toilets and baths, and so on. Sheds, workshops and gardens all varied and matured. By the 1960s, DIY and renovation were commencing (thank you Barry Bucknell), paint colours were more varied, windows styles were changing, as were roofing types. TV aerials proliferated, pebbledash began to appear on walls, and there were more cars on the streets. Modelling detail and variety in sympathy with your targeted time period can add much more depth and credibility to your layout.

The artistic use of a *trompe l'oeil* is a great way of portraying depth in an urban landscape. Here the road fools the eye as the transition from horizontal to vertical is assisted by a wooden angle blended in behind the telephone box. The mixed media painting of the rear wall and the ruined warehouse accompanied by the forward-scene details of the gates and wired fencing soften the backboard.

*Above*: A different technique is used here, at the far end of the bridge, to carry the eye. Low relief buildings are combined with oblique angled print images on the board behind. Cleverly, Graham Hobbs has foreshortened the embankment and the road behind and varied the fencing to break up the mind's expectations. When watching a goods train clatter by at this point the eye is well and truly fooled.

*Below*: Low relief rear-of-house kits are available, such as these from Metcalfe. Some detail differences are supplied with the kits, but a bit of kit-bashing from spares or broken kits can add to the variety, as seen in the right-hand image. Variation can make the mundane into an art form. Over time you can build up a rich spares box of materials, surface textures and features that can all be reused.

## Isolated Grand Buildings in an Urban Setting

As a town or city grows it subsumes independent houses and land within it. Sometimes buildings are demolished, land is cleared, and all that remains is a name, an old tree, an out-of-place wall. At other times buildings survive and take on new uses: commercial offices, multiple occupancy dwellings or some other purpose such as a doctor's surgery. All this provides an excuse for the railway modeller to import something grand in nature and indulge in some architectural fancy.

On the Club Market Obthorpe 7mm O gauge layout there is a scenic end beyond the terminal station. In order to maintain interest and bring features to the eye, the Station Road approach winds round a rising hill. This provided the opportunity to incorporate a Georgian house with a basement, accentuating the vertical dimension but not dominating it. In the Wroxeter Roman Road layout constructed by the author there is a 'winter gardens', which the Victorians would have classed as a 'grand glass entertainments palace'. This is loosely based on the opera house at Buxton and is a low relief skyline feature to give an idea of depth. To reinforce the existence of this feature, buses in the area carry adverts for upcoming appearances. Department stores are another good addition, giving a feel for the heart of a town or city, especially in low relief as a backdrop to the railway.

We must not ignore the grand feature of the railway station itself. Such buildings were often built way out of any scale appropriate to the location or financial profitability, as flights of fancy for the investors. Euston started this trend in 1838 and the years of 'railway mania' ensured it continued.

*Above*: A Lincolnshire example of a gentleman farmer's residence that once was an outlier of a settlement but is now swallowed up by more modern growth. Picking on the vernacular style of older buildings for the region being modelled is important as it rewards the modeller with a cohesive feeling on completion.

*Opposite above left*: This is an MDF laser-cut low relief building in O by Petite Properties. These allow a choice of reskinning options for the final finish, in this case laser-printed bricks of custom design. MDF of the same thickness is used to define the forward basement area and it will be given iron railings from the Peco Lineside range.

*Opposite above right*: The aim is not to copy a prototype here but to incorporate enough regional style to be convincing on the Club's Lincolnshire themed Market Obthorpe layout. The building is seen here nearing completion and having a lightbox test. Once dropped below the roadside paving at the rear of the hilltop on the scenic board, it will appear to be taller but not dominate the model.

## Urban Grit: The Priory in N

The Priory is a diorama constructed from donated and recovered materials. It is proportioned so that the railway element was under 20% of the display area. N gauge lends itself to big sweeps of the brush in design. A railway lost in nothingness, wandering through an open country setting is impressive. Losing the railway in urban confusion is the diametric opposite, but also works well in this scale.

This layout has been extended to bring in the feel of a northern English town tucked into surrounding mills and industry, almost as if the buildings were as a wave breaking on a beach. It is not yet a full working layout, more a vignette to experiment with techniques and the aim is to link it to a display loop as part of a larger entity.

While the ideal is to add extra detailing, using the same off-the-shelf kits en masse can achieve an overall feeling of a Victorian expanded town. With its back alleys and unforgiving industrial edifices looming in the background, it gets you looking for the original Rovers Return tucked away on a corner.

The priory ruin itself will be situated on a watercourse on the other side of the railway link, as shown on the overall plan for the layout extension, and will be a 3D-printed entity.

Some general urban planning is needed (unlike the prototype townscape which would grow organically until real controls came into local government). It helps to give names to roads and factories as conversations about tasking and problems become targeted. If you are the sole builder of your town, it gives a real sense of ownership to name everything. On this board we have just the one tree and some allotments. Green relief will come in phase two when the loop line will be hidden under the limestone cragged Priory Hill.

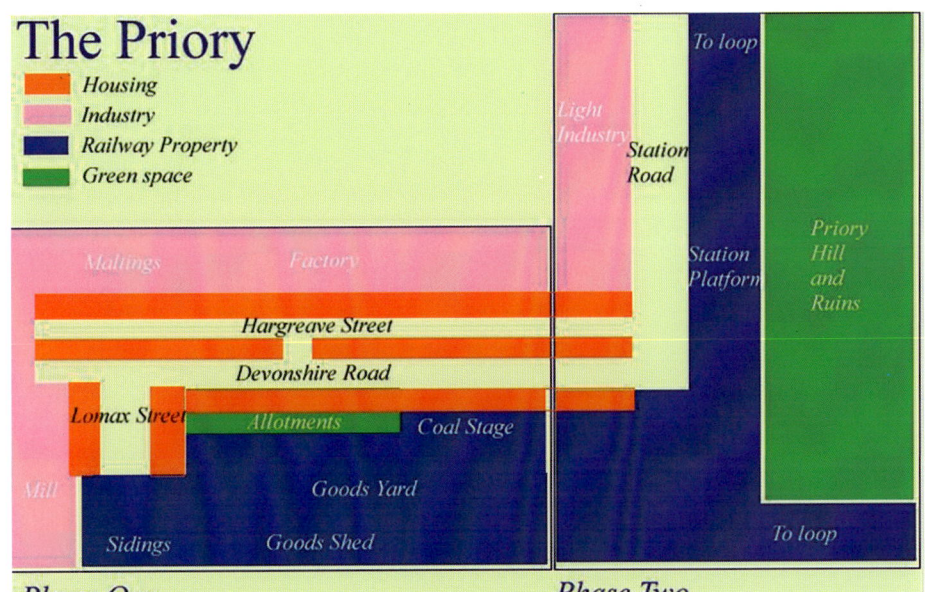

A bird's eye view of the current phase one unexpanded town. It is in effect a siding, goods yard and unforgiving hard-hit crowded urban community set in the decline of traditional industry in the early 1960s. The right-hand side will contain the main rail loop and the priory ruin itself. As a differentiator to many layouts the view of the station will be short side on to the viewer, giving the railway a secondary role to the town rather than dominating the scene.

The mix of factories and terraces can suit just about any location in Britain that experienced a Victorian expansion phase. South London, Basingstoke, Bradford or Reading all have their expansion areas. This means that your regionality for the railway need not be the driving factor for your actual buildings. In moving materials the length and breadth of the country, the railway enabled a migration from the vernacular into homogeneous housing stock. Devonshire Road and Lomax Street around the mill and goods shed are comprised of older grey brick buildings. Coming a bit later, Hargreave Street (named after the inventor of the Spinning Jenny) is in red brick.

Dirty old town. The view out of the window of a Waterloo-bound commuter train from Teddington in March 1963 looking over the Nine Elms tracks to Victoria and Battersea Power Station. Railway, industry, housing and blight, all in one evocative image. Battersea was not actually completed in four-chimney format until 1955. The majority of coal came from colliers on the Thames rather than using the close rail links. (*Gordon Farrow*)

The goods facility dominates but is balanced by the urban sprawl rising behind. BR Standard 2-6-0 4MT 76069 backs slowly into the goods shed as a Scammel mechanical horse trundles around with an outbound container load. The aim of this part of the layout is to keep it mundane and ordinary, as an anchor for the hill module.

Devonshire Road leading to James Sheffield's mill. Can you smell the coal smoke? Chimney pots are always being damaged so we will experiment with 3D-printed alternatives.

Looking along the yard to Lomax Street. The join plate between phase one and two is at the bottom. The 'balanced house' is deliberate – to hide joins on portable boards it can be useful to have detachable buildings which are placed over them once set up.

# 11
# Industrial Buildings

*Above and right*: Heavy industry as a backdrop to your layout adds a layer of reality to your model as traditionally the railway would attract and then service such installations. Here 4-4-2T LTSR Whitelegg Tilbury Tank 41967 pulls a down train consisting of ancient empty coaching stock (ECS), passing the BPCM Wouldham Cement (Lion) Works at West Thurrock in the pouring rain on 29 December 1951. (*Online Transport Archive Meredith 235-2*)

The industrial scene is a great space filler on a layout. Corners that would otherwise be empty can be given vertical arrangements of chimneys, silos and pipework. Backscenes to sidings can be given a low relief reason for existence. For example, such subjects as coal mining conveyors and screens to load trucks, an oil depot made from cut tin cans or plastic tubs, or a town gas and coke facility.

Any industry in the real would that would require bulk delivery or a mass despatch in the past would be likely to have sidings and traffic.

## Things to Consider for Industrial Scenes

- Either have chimneys as demountable, or ensure they are embedded into the baseboard. Otherwise stray arm movements will break your model.
- It is tempting to have crisp sharp edges, especially if the materials being used are thin metals, so observe safety first in construction and ensure you cannot injure yourself during or indeed, afterwards.
- If running lines enter a building, ensure you have the ability to remove the building to clean the track and also rerail stock following any incident.
- Modern facilities tend towards a clean and tidy finish, often imposed by law. Older buildings and yards benefit from clutter and an application of dirt/weathering. Products such as 'Dirty Down' spray are used by film and diorama specialists to achieve this grimy finish.
- If using a standard kit in a low relief situation, think of how best to slice it, to double up a frontage.
- The image of a brickworks in a corner of Graham Hobbs's layout shows a structure typical of the Peterborough area. The smoke is a great finishing touch.

## Alville Yard East in HO

Alville Yard East is a portable layout by Club member Alan Hancock. American outline HO enables large rolling stock examples to be fitted into a small space, especially where older industrial areas are portrayed. Here the layout imparts the feel of a canyon through the city. A mix of tall, low relief warehouses and smaller commercial blocks gives a typical mid-American city feel.

Including decaying survivors of a previous grandeur gives this 1957 portrayal a true stateside atmosphere. Keeping the colour palette carefully to washed mid-tones was part of the trick to impart a cohesive 'faded photograph' feel throughout.

The buildings are a mix of plaster, resin, plastic and wood. The board itself is kept generally lightweight to compensate, as this is a layout capable of being taken to exhibitions.

*Above*: Cleverly drawing the eye by rotating the upper-level railroad into a static scene aimed at the viewer. The buildings here are examples of American outline models in plastic, resin and white metal.

*Opposite above*: Low relief steel framed buildings with brick skins allow a variety of colours and angles. Their blocky nature blends in with the scenic flat of tower blocks and skyscrapers on the backboard.

INDUSTRIAL BUILDINGS • 93

The canyon-like sides act as an ideal scene for emphasising the super detailed quality of American HO railroad cars and locomotives. There is always room for a grounded caboose body for that final touch.

Despite being a land of open spaces, American high land values in cities have forced multi-level constructions for industrial and commercial areas, making these ideal for small modelling spaces. Seen here is New York Long Island, near the 21st Street Van Alst station, in May 2001, demonstrating the same blocky steel frame construction and canyon-like feel. (*Author*)

# Gracetown Bank by Graham Moorfoot

We crossed paths with Graham at a South Lincolnshire model show and were very taken with his layout. He is a local who has produced a northern valley-based industrial complex full of innovative ideas in a small area.

Clutter, weeds and well detailed and coloured low relief buildings with lots of detail add to the scenic values. The 4 x 2ft (122 x 60cm) baseboard makes use of standard OO code 100 Peco track and includes a crossover and a rope-worked inclined bank at the rear. Fiddle yards of 2ft (60cm) exist offstage at either side. Magnets below the track allow hands-free shunting in conjunction with Kadee couplers on the rolling stock.

*Above, left and bottom left*: This layout makes use of a backscene of low relief industrial buildings which are overtopped by the green summit of the valley sides. The buildings retain their interest by the clever use of the inclined embankment to draw the eye forward of them. What could be a dead area becomes part of the overall depth of focus. The layout shows that with an industrial landscape you can fit a lot of interest in without it appearing cluttered. It retains operational interest with small locos powering individual wagons and vans into meaningful positions. Planning your building positions for perspective, together with judicious positioning, brings the rewards of 'little reveals' as the eye follows movement.

Nenthead in O gauge, with a paper mill on an outdoor section. The external boards on this model railway are demountable, only appearing outside in good summer weather. Heavy industry with larger buildings shows up well in such settings. Skytrex resin is used for the general fabric as it tolerates expansion with the changes in heat as the sun hits the buildings. (*Paul Bason*/Railway Modeller)

*Above left, above right and right*: The industrial section of our GNR EM gauge layout Woodcroft incorporates a narrow gauge wharfage section to add operational interest plus brick ovens consuming a coal supply. These are scratch built and also interesting in that a scaffold pole smashed an acute diagonal over the buildings partially destroying them during the Club exhibition vandalism. They were effectively stitched back together by talented members and infilled to make an almost seamless repair. The light and dark brickwork variation, viewed from a distance, now adds to their mystique.

## Making a Small Footprint Look Imposing

Unless you are basing your layout within a facility such as coal mine sidings, an oil refinery, a brewery or a dockyard, you will be bringing industrial buildings in piecemeal, as space fillers. If you picture a journey by train on a main line, from your carriage window view you have many faceless and unidentifiable industrial buildings around you. Pipework, railings and strange roof lines abound and the occasional name of a company flashes by.

The scratch-built iron casting house on Butterwick in O gauge represents just such a factory. Loosely based on the Coalbrookdale area, the specialist castings floor would have air and water feeds from outside. The company name of Benthall Works is proudly emblazoned on the outside but the grandness is offset by ugly pipes punching out from the original Victorian brickwork and spoiling the symmetry.

It was decided to use a slight offset on these two buildings to combine with the curving backscene to give a feeling of greater depth.

The factory carcase used a wood beading and fibreboard as the core structure, topped with Daler art board for the roof stiffener. This makes it easy to cut through to position the windows onto the back of plastic brick sheet. This also forms a lightbox for internal illumination.

Once the window furniture is in place and a brick wash applied to the outside using acrylics, it is time to add lettering and a pediment. If you space out your activities you can determine when best to paint and at what level of detail, before completing.

*Above*: Brickwork completed and 3D-printed lettering in place. The next step was to manipulate the 'Y' axis stretch on 3D-printable pipes. The pipes were sourced online as creative commons from thingiverse.com and were originally for a Warhammer outer-space diorama. These were painted in twentieth-century finishes – mid-powder blue for water and gas pipes and a dull aluminium metallic colour for the air supply and venting pipes.

*Below*: The best time to test finishes, position details and undertake light tests is when the building is on the workbench. Once fixed on a layout it can become a nightmare to remedy anything accidentally left out of the project.

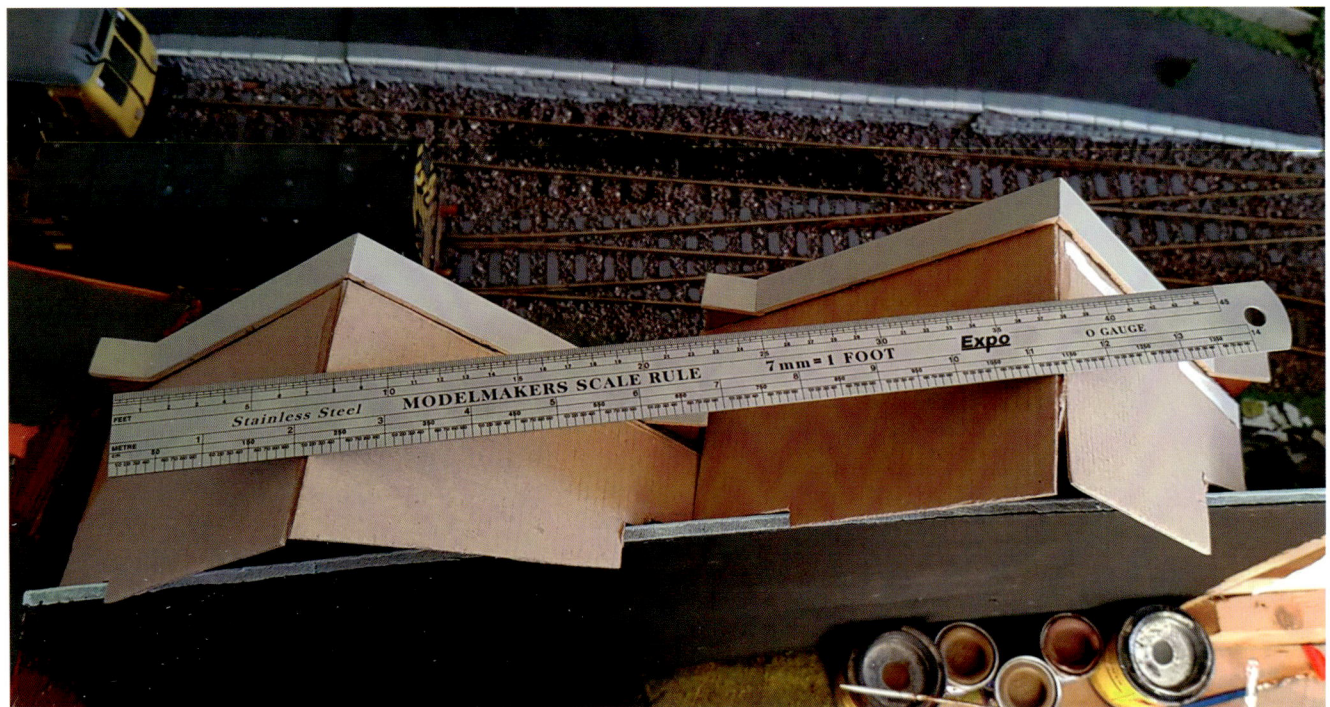

*Above*: Offered up to determine the best extension of the roofline. The outer card of cat/dog food pouch boxes is very stiff and provides a cheap (and green) material in scratch building for indoor locations. Seen here is the trusty modelmaker's steel ruler. They exist for the majority of scales and are ideal for testing your decisions in size against a 6ft human in a prototype image or from some other recognisable item in shot which is scalable.

*Left*: Roofing with slates. You can buy pre-embossed plasticard with slates or tiles to use like a brick sheet – it cuts out a lot of fuss and is comparatively fast. The rooflines of the Euston model used printed brick papers with a 3D-printed ridge feature. For this factory building the fine card method was chosen to get the correct look and feel. While the purist may construct a frame, add laths and then place each slate (wargaming-damaged buildings look great with this), here a speedier technique was used with postcard-thickness card.

INDUSTRIAL BUILDINGS • 99

The desired slate size was drawn up, allowing for overlaps and a sharp craft knife was used to cut 75% of the distance, leaving solid at the overlap line. A knife is preferable to scissors as cutting with the two blades curls the slates away from flatness. Once painted this will be accentuated. The occasional positioning of a broken or missing slate also adds nicely to the end product.

Benthall Works main building in finished form. Cream ridge tiles would have had a slip glaze of Jackfield factory origin. The 3D-printed lineside walls lost their railings in the war, but rusted stubs are still showing. A little research of your chosen geographical area combined with a timeline gives buildings a grounded, vernacular theme.

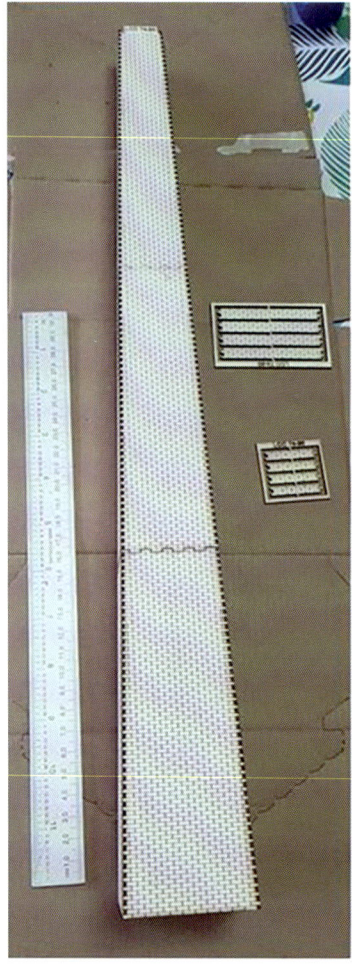

*Above left:* Assembling a laser-cut card kit from LCUT Creative. The technique is simple enough, combining sides using the crenelated edge cut-outs. However, you do need to coax these into place to avoid damaging the surface paper.
*Above middle:* Once the glue has dried it is time for painting. We mixed high quality matt emulsion test pots to get the desired hue. The paints have a good opacity of pigment for the thin application required to preserve the brick/mortar laser embossing. *Above right:* Once the paint had had a day to set adequately, we used watered-down acrylics applied with a broad artist's brush. Finally, a damp scrap cloth was used to swiftly rub the new application layer off, leaving mortar in place and aiding the weathering of bricks.

*Left*: A couple of iron supporting straps applied using black card gives the impression of strength. Spraying with Dirty Down spray as a final touch completed the build.

# Why We 'Do' Model Railways

With the help of Warners/*BRM* magazine and Sleaford MRC we built a foldable layout for the Little Miracles Cerebral Palsy charity and added track and scenery over a single show weekend in 2019. The act of running a model railway is in itself very therapeutic.

The hobby is good for personal therapy, bringing calm, control, and generally assisting good mental health in building, running and learning. This photo taken alongside a BBC *Look North* camera team is where my wife said, 'It is cute'. I may forgive her one day!

This hobby enables mixing between age groups and skill sets. Here are the degree students from Hertfordshire University who were designing and printing elements for the *Dream Big* movie, with the result seen at Miniatura 2021.

You get to meet great people with a common interest. Here is a busy Club night ahead of the annual Stamford exhibition 2022.